Ancient Monuments
&
Historical Sites

BROCKHAMPTON PRESS
LONDON

This edition published 1997 by Brockhampton Press, a member of the
Hodder Headline PLC Group

ISBN 1 86019 725 6

Printed and bound in India

Introduction

This is an A-Z guide to the ancient monuments and historic sites of Britain and Northern Ireland. There are a great many such sites and the guide includes a wide selection of the more important ones. The sites are listed A-Z by name.

This introduction includes a brief history of Britain so that the events and dates mentioned can be read in context.

Britain has been inhabited by people for the best part of half a million years but the earliest evidence of human life dates from 250,000 BC. Around 5000 BC, at the thawing of the last Ice Age, the British Isles separated from mainland Europe. In about 3500 BC, new colonists arrived in Britain from Europe bringing Neolithic culture. These tribes cleared forests, enclosed fields and constructed defensive ditches round their villages. They also mined for flint, which they used to make tools and pottery. Many graves—stone-chambered, turf-covered mounds—remain from this period.

In around 2000 BC, the Neolithic period gave way to the Bronze Age with the immigration of the Beaker Folk from northern Europe. These people originated in the Iberian peninsula and brought with them bronze workers from the Rhineland. These people lived in an organized structure with established hierarchies and quickly integrated with the native population. Many of the stone circles of Britain were built during this period, as were many earthwork forts.

In about 600 BC, Celtic invaders came to Britain from central Europe. The Celts were skilled in battle and soon overpowered the native inhabitants. They established a farming economy and a social structure that was led by the Druids who were knowledgeable about ritual, legend and the gods. The Celts introduced metalworking with iron rather than bronze and worked with gold for ornamental pieces. The Celts also introduced many hillforts or brochs and other defensive works. The Celtic tongue gradually divided into Goidelic (Q-Celtic), which is now spoken in Ireland and Scotland, and Brythonic (P-Celtic), which is spoken in Cornwall, Wales and Brittany in France.

The Roman invasion of Britain began in 55 BC, with Julius Caesar making hestitant cross-Channel excursions. The Romans were keen to invade Britain to stop the collaboration between the British Celts and the French anti-Roman tribes. In August AD 43, the Roman emperor Claudius ordered his troops to land in Kent following the death of the British king, Cunobelin. The force soon established a base along the estuary of the Thames. Within four years the Romans had spread and were dug in on the frontier of south Wales.

Until AD 50, when he was betrayed and captured, Caratacus, the Catuvellauni chief, conducted a guerrilla campaign from Wales. Ten years later the Romans were challenged by the East Anglian Iceni, under their queen Boudicca (Boadicea), who sacked Camulodunum and Verulamium and reached as far as the port of Londinium. This uprising was soon quashed and was an isolated incident. Wales and the north of England were not subdued until AD 79.

In AD 80, Agricola began an invasion of the north that involved building a string of defences across the Clyde-Forth line and defeating a large force of Scottish tribes at Mons Graupius. This campaign, however, was ill-fated and in AD 123 Emperor Hadrian decided to seal off the northern tribes by building Hadrian's Wall, which stretched from the Solway Firth to the Tyne. This construction represented the first formal division of mainland Britain. Twenty years later the Romans built the Antonine Wall between the Clyde and the Forth and this was occupied for forty years. After this the Romans decided to leave the north and introduced a policy of containment.

The Romans ruled for nearly four hundred years and began a written history of Britain. England was unified and peaceful and commerce flourished. Cities prospered, in particular Londinium, which had a central role. Roman and Celtic traditions coexisted and many people worshipped Celtic and Roman gods. The Romans also introduced Christianity to Britain from the 3rd century on.

By the start of the 5th century, England had become detached from the Roman Empire and within fifty years the Saxons began settling in Britain. There was much resistance to the Saxons, led by such semi-mythical figures as King Arthur, but the Britons were defeated in 577 at the Battle of Dyrham at which three British kings were killed. The remaining Celtic tribes moved to Cumbria, Wales and the West Country. The Saxons eliminated Romano-British culture and established the Anglo-Saxon kingdoms of Northumbria, Mercia, East Anglia, Kent and Wessex.

Celtic traditions survived in Scotland and Wales where the tribes were untouched by Roman or Teutonic invaders. In the 5th century, Irish-Celtic invaders formed colonies in areas of Wales and Scotland. Between the 6th and 8th centuries the Celtic saints spread the gospel around Ireland and the west of Britain. These saints promoted the tradition of living a reclusive life. St David was the most popular in south Wales and in Scotland St Columba founded many Christian outposts.

The arrival of St Augustine in England saw the revival of Christianity. Augustine was given permission to found a monastery at Canterbury where the king was baptised, followed by ten thousand of his subjects, at a Christmas ceremony. England was quickly Christianized, and by the middle of the 7th century all the Anglo-Saxon kings were Christian.. There were clashes between the Augustinian missionaries and the Celtic monks. These were resolved by the Synod of Whitby in 663 when it was established that the English church should follow the rule of Rome.

The dominant Anglo-Saxon kingdom during the 8th century was Mercia, which was ruled by the kings Ethelbald and Offa. Offa ordered the construction of Offa's Dyke. This was the greatest public work of the Anglo-Saxon period and was an earthwork that stretched from the River Dee to the Severn marking the border between England and Wales. After Offa's death, Wessex became the dominant kingdom and by 825 had conquered or formed allegiances with all the other English kingdoms.

During this period the first large-scale Norse or Danish Viking invasions began with coastal pirate raids. One such raid destroyed the monastery of Lindisfarne in 793. The Vikings migrated to the Scottish islands of Orkney and Shetland and the Hebrides.

In 865 substantial Danish forces landed in East Anglia, and within six years Northumbria, Mercia and East Anglia had been conquered and Wessex was under attack. At this time Wessex was under the leadership of Alfred the Great, who realized the need to coexist with the Danes and so established a border between his domain from the northern Danelaw.

In 899, Alfred's successor, Edward the Elder, established supremacy over the Danelaw and was then the overlord of all England. His rule was even acknowledged by Scottish and Welsh chieftains. The first crowned king of England was Edgar, king of Mercia and Northumberland, in 973. The Danes continued to be aggressive, and in 1016 Ethelred the Unready fled to Normandy and established allegiances there.

Canute was the first and best king of the short-lived Danish dynasty. He was followed by two sons but after them the Saxons were restored under Ethelred's son, Edward the Confessor. After Edward died, Harold was named king but this was disputed by William, Duke of Normandy, who claimed that Edward had promised him the succession. Harold's reign was short-lived and in its ten-month period he had to fend off an invasion by his brother Tostig in league with the King Harald of Norway. Following his return from this victory, Harold had to face the invading troops of William at the Battle of Hastings in 1066. Harold was killed at this battle and William the Conqueror was installed as king at Westminster Abbey.

William I imposed a new military aristocracy on his subjects and enforced his rule with a series of strongholds throughout England, the most impressive of which was the Tower of London. Rebellions were ruthlessly quashed by a scorched earth policy. The Domesday Book was compiled between 1085 and 1086, and it recorded land ownership, type of cultivation, the number of inhabitants and their social status. This information was used to provide a framework for taxation, judicial structure and feudal obligations.

In 1087 William was succeeded by his son, William Rufus, who was a benefactor of religious foundations and was killed by an arrow while hunting in the New Forest. Henry I, William's youngest son, was the next king, and he married a Saxon princess. Henry I died in 1135 and his daughter Mathilda's accession was contested by Stephen of Blois, William I's grandson. The nineteen years of his reign saw England at civil war. Mathilda's son was eventually considered Stephen's heir, and so began the reign of Henry II, the first of the Plataganet branch

of the Norman line. Henry II implemented administrative re-
forms and introduced trial by jury. In 1170 he sanctioned the
murder of Thomas à Becket in Canterbury Cathedral in an attempt to subordinate ecclesiastical authority.

Henry II was father to Richard I (Richard Lionheart) who
spent most of his ten-year reign at the crusades in the Holy
Land. Richard's brother, King John, consented to a charter guar-
anteeing the rights and privileges of the barons. This was known
as the Magna Carta and was signed in 1215. The barons' struggle for power continued into the reign of Henry III who was defeated by Simon de Montfort, leader of the barons, at Lewes in
1265. At this time both Henry III and Prince Edward were taken
prisoner. Edward escaped, defeated the barons and went on to
become Edward I in 1272. Edward presided over the Model
Parliament of 1295 but was primarily concerned with extending
his kingdom by annexing Wales and imposing English jurisdic-
tion in Scotland.

Wales was not annexed by William the Conqueror. He installed a huge retinue of barons, the Lords Marcher, along the
border in an attempt to gain control over more Welsh territory.
Despite local protests, the barons maintained their privileges up
until Henry VIII's Act of Union four hundred years later.

Edward I's succession saw an irrevocable change in the rela-
tionship between England and Wales. Edward I was determined
to unify Britain. Edward was able to push the Welsh chief
Llewelyn back into Snowdonia. The Treaty of Aberconwy restored peace but stripped Llywelyn of all but the title 'Prince of
Wales'. Four years later, Dafydd, Llywelyn's brother, rose up
against Edward but the revolt was crushed and Llywelyn was
executed.

In 1284 the Treaty of Rhuddlan set down the terms by which
Wales was to be governed by an English monarch. In 1294 there

was a rebellion led by Madog ap Llywelyn, but this was halted by Edward I.

In 1400 Owain Glyndwr declared himself 'Prince of Wales' and along with a crew of supporters attacked the land of the barons and slaughtered the English. Glyndwr's support grew as a result of the restrictions imposed by Henry IV. In 1404 a parliament was summoned in Machynlleth by Glyndwr who was crowned Prince of Wales. He then demanded independence for Wales but then suffered a series of defeats and the rebellion had lost momentum by 1408.

In 1057 Malcolm III (Canmore) defeated Macbeth and this saw the beginning of change in Scottish society. Malcolm III had spent seventeen years at the English court and sought to apply much of what he had seen there to Scotland. He introduced succession through the male line and feudalism, which was diametrically opposed to the Gaelic system. The Canmores feudalized much of southern and eastern Scotland but beyond these areas clan-based societies persisted.

The Canmores began to reform the Church. This was initiated by Malcolm's English wife, Margaret, and was continued by David I who imported monks to found a series of monasteries. The dynasty also founded a series of royal burghs such as Edinburgh, Stirling and Berwick. The Gaelic-speaking clans had no real importance in these burghs and by 1550 Scots had become the main language of lowland Scotland.

The changes made by the Canmores resulted in a rift between the Highland and Lowland communities. They were united against the threat from the south and Edward I. Rival claimants to the Scottish throne presented themselves to Edward I, and John Balliol was chosen above Robert the Bruce. Bruce did not accept this decision and conflict continued. In 1295 Balliol renounced his allegiance with Edward and formed an alliance with France—the beginning of the Auld Alliance. Bruce sided with the English, Balliol was defeated and Edward seized control of most of Scotland.

William Wallace formed an army of peasants, lesser nobles and townsmen to resist the atrocities of Edward I and to fight for independence. Wallace was never supported by the nobles and was eventually betrayed and executed in London in 1305.

In 1306 Robert the Bruce defied Edward and crowned himself king of Scotland. Edward died in 1307, but the unrest did not end until Bruce defeated the English army, led by Edward II, at the Battle of Bannockburn in 1314. In 1320 the Scots asserted their right to independence in a petition to the pope known as the Arbroath Declaration.

Edward II was later overthrown by his wife, Isabella, and her lover, Roger Mortimer. Edward III, the son of Edward II and Isabella, made a claim to the throne of France, and this saw the beginning of the Hundred Years War in 1337. The early English victories were interrupted by the outbreak of the Black Death in 1349, which killed about a third of the English population. The resulting economic turmoil resulted in the Peasants' Revolt in 1381. The rebels were dispersed after the murder of their leader, Wat Tyler, and terrible retribution followed.

In 1399 Richard II was overthrown by John de Gaunt's son who took the title Henry IV and founded the Lancastrian dynasty. He was succeeded fourteen years later by his son, Henry V, who renewed the war with France and forced the French king to sign the Treaty of Troyes in 1420, which made the English king the heir to the French throne. Joan of Arc beat back the English, and by 1454 only Calais was left in English hands.

The War of the Roses broke out a year after the last English garrisons returned from France. In 1450 Jack Cade's Rebellion challenged the authority of the king and won a battle at

Sevenoaks before being dispersed. Henry VI and his wife were overthrown by the son of Richard, Duke of York, who was crowned Edward IV in 1461—the first king of the Yorkist line.

Richard Neville, Earl of Warwick, formed an allegiance with Margaret of Anjou, the wife of the former king, Henry VI, and forced Edward IV into exile and Henry VI was once again proclaimed king. In 1471 Edward returned after the Battle of Barnet and captured Margaret and murdered Henry's heir. Henry himself was sent to the Tower.

Edward IV was succeeded by Edward V, but he and his younger brother were murdered in the Tower of London—they are thought to have been killed by their uncle, the Duke of Gloucester, who was crowned Richard III but was defeated at Bosworth Field in 1485 by Henry Tudor, Earl of Richmond, who was later crowned Henry VII.

Henry VII unified Lancastrian and Yorkist factions by marrying Edward IV's daughter, Elizabeth. England became more affluent and increased in importance in Europe. Henry VII's daughter married James IV of Scotland and his son married Catherine, daughter of Ferdinand and Isabella of Spain.

Henry VIII succeeded to the throne in 1509. His reign is noted for the separation of the English Church from Rome. This was triggered by Henry VIII's desire for a decree of nullity for his marriage to Catherine of Aragon, which was refused by Rome. He forced the English Church to recognize him as the head of the Church. Henry VIII instigated the dissolution of the monasteries in 1536. Henry VIII was married six times but had only one male heir who took the throne as Edward VI in 1547 aged nine. Under his reign Protestantism was firmly established and churches were stripped of images and Catholic services were banned. On Edward's death, his half-sister Mary was recognized by most of the country to be the heir to the throne and she restored England to the papacy and married the future Philip II of Spain. This resulted in a war with France and England lost Calais. Mary began a persecution of the Protestants and became increasingly unpopular.

In 1558, Elizabeth I, Mary's half-sister and a Protestant, took the throne during a time when the country was divided in religious loyalties. During Elizabeth's reign there was an English Renaissance, the highlight of which was the career of William Shakespeare. There were also many famous seafarers at this time, including Walter Raleigh, Francis Drake, Martin Frobisher and John Hawkins. In 1588 the English navy defeated the Spanish Armada.

During the War of the Roses the Welsh allegiances lay with the Lancastrians, who were supported by the north Welsh Tewdwr family. The Welsh had high hopes for the first Tudor monarch, Henry VII, and he lived up to some of them—he lifted many of the restrictions on land ownership and promoted many Welshmen to high office but the power was still held by the Crown and the Marcher lords. A uniform administrative structure was reached under Henry VIII.

The Acts of Union in 1536 and 1543 fixed English sovereignty over Wales. The Marches were replaced by shires and England and Wales shared legal equality. The break from native traditions was not widely appreciated, and many Welsh people remained poor and were not able to speak English—the language of the law.

Protestantism was readily received in Wales during the reign of Henry VIII. The Bible was translated into Welsh during the Reformation by William Morgan. The gap between the rich and poor widened in Wales during this period as some gentry benefited from the dissolution of the monasteries.

Bruce died in 1329 and the Scottish monarchy declined in influence following his death. The last heir of the Bruce dynasty died in 1371 and was succeeded by the 'Stewards'—Stewarts. A succession of Scottish rulers took the throne while they were children. The last of these was James VI in 1567. The Scottish nobles took advantage of the power vacuum and exercised control over Scotland's affairs. The Scottish suffered a terrible defeat to the English under the reign of James IV at Flodden Field.

Mary Queen of Scots reigned from 1542–67, coming to the throne aged just one week. Henry VIII wanted Mary to marry his son, Edward, and he tried to enforce this with his military might. From 1544 the English launched an attack on Scotland until the Scottish turned to the Auld Alliance for support. Mary was to marry the dauphin, Francis, in return for military assistance from France. Mary sailed for France in 1548. Her husband took the French throne in 1559 but died thirteen years later, at which time Mary returned to Scotland.

By the end of the 16th century, the Church was held in contempt by the Scottish people and the resentment of French influences spurred the Reformation and Protestantism. In 1557 the Lords of the Congregation formed to promote Protestantism. The Scottish Parliament asserted the primacy of Protestantism, forbidding Catholic services and denouncing the authority of the pope.

Mary's marriage to her second husband, Lord Darnley, was disastrous. He murdered her friend David Rizzio and in 1567 Darnley himself was murdered. Soon after this Mary married the Earl of Bothwell—whom many believed had murdered Darnley. After this the Scots rebelled and Mary was driven into exile in England. Her son, James, was left behind to be raised as a Protestant prince. Mary was perceived as a threat to the English throne and was executed on the orders of Elizabeth I in 1587.

John Knox then reformed the kirk, which adopted a Presbyterian structure administered by a hierarchy of assemblies, part elected and part appointed. James VI disliked Presbyterianism because of the lack of royally appointed bishops and felt that the kirk threatened his authority. In 1610 he was installed as the king of England, and he was then able to install Scottish bishops.

James VI of Scotland became James I of England and so the English and Scottish crowns were united. James moved to end hostilities with Spain, actions that were resented by English Protestants. James's tolerance towards Catholics was thwarted in 1605 by the Gunpowder Plot when Guy Fawkes and a group of Catholic conspirators were found plotting to blow up the king and Parliament.

There was an inevitable split between James VI and I and the landed gentry. James VI and I strongly believed in the divine right of kings but the landed gentry were strongly represented in Parliament, which was becoming increasingly powerful. The split was deepened by the persecution of the Puritans. The king chose to stand back from the Parliamentarians and relied on his court advisers.

The second Stuart king (the later Stuarts adopted the spelling Stuart rather than Stewart) was Charles I, who was raised in Episcopalian England and had little understanding of Scottish reformism. He also had a strong belief in the divine right of kings and in 1637 he attempted to impose a new prayer book on the Scottish Kirk, which was in line with the practices of the High Anglican Church. The reformers denounced these changes and organized the National Covenant, which was committed to recovering the purity and liberty of the gospel. Charles declared the Covenanters rebels. The king backed down from military action, and the General Assembly of the Kirk abolished the episcopacy. Although Charles declared these actions illegal, he lacked the finances to organize a military campaign sufficient to fight the well-funded Covenanters.

Charles I reacted by calling the first English Parliament in eleven years but found criticism rather than support. In 1642 Charles withdrew to Nottingham after acknowledging the increased hostility of the Parliament. He raised his standard there and so began the Civil War. The Royalists were initially more powerful than the Parliamentarian army. However, Oliver Cromwell overhauled the Parliamentarian army and the tables began to turn. Charles was captured by the Scots in 1646 and handed over to the English. He was eventually executed in 1649.

In 1650 the future Charles II was invited to Scotland to regain his Scottish kingdom by renouncing his father and signing the Covenant. This 'Presbyterian restoration' was not to last long. Cromwell invaded Scotland and the Scots were defeated at Dunbar. Charles was forced into exile as a result. The next eleven years saw the whole of Britain as a Commonwealth. After three years as a republic, a protectorate under Cromwell was established. Cromwell was an impatient and arbitrary leader who was infamous for his harsh policies in Ireland. He died in 1658 and after a brief period of rule by his son, Richard, Parliament voted to restore the monarchy and Charles II became king.

Charles's reign brought about the Restoration, and this was warmly welcomed following the turmoil of the previous twenty years. His reign also encompassed the Great Plague and the Great Fire of London. There were still tensions between the king and Parliament at this time.

In 1685 the Catholic James II (VII of Scotland), brother of Charles II, succeeded to the throne, but there was much opposition and the Duke of Monmouth (Charles's illegitimate son)

challenged the king. This was unsuccessful and he was executed in 1685. Many suspected sympathisers and rebels were
also executed or deported.

James II incurred further protests by removing anti-Catholic
restrictions and stating his intention to raise his son a Catholic.
James II's Protestant daughter Mary was married to the Dutch
William of Orange who was informed of the unrest. He arrived
in Devon and was declared king after the Glorious Revolution—the final episode of the Civil War.

William and Mary were joint sovereigns and they defined the
limitations of the powers of the monarchy. Mary died in 1694
and William continued to rule alone. He used England to defend
Holland from France, and this stance defined England's political status in Europe for the next sixty years. William and Mary
did not have an heir so the crown was passed to Mary's sister,
Anne, who had several children, none of whom survived childhood. Parliament instigated the Act of Settlement in 1701,
which barred Catholics or anyone married to a Catholic from
succession to the English throne. As a result of this, the
Electress Sophia of Hanover was named as the successor to the
throne. The Act of Settlement did not apply in Scotland, and
there were concerns that the Scottish would ask James II' son,
James Edward Stuart, to return from France and be their king.

In spite of anti-English feeling, the Act of Union was passed
by the Scottish Parliament in 1707. This guaranteed free trade
between Scotland and England and the independence of the
Scottish legal system and the Presbyterian Kirk. The new Parliament was to be based in London.

In 1714 Anne died and the succession passed to the German
Duke of Hanover, George I. This was the trigger for the first
Jacobite uprising, which supported James Edward Stuart's
claim to the throne. The Scottish people were becoming disillu-

sioned with the Union, and many English people also supported the right of the Stuarts above the German-speaking George I. In 1715 the Stuart standard was raised at Braemar Castle by John Erskine, Earl of Mar, and eight days later he captured Perth. From here he raised a 10,000-strong army. The rebellion lacked decisive action and lost the advantage of surprise. By the time James arrived, Dutch troops had been drafted in and the rebellion disintegrated. James was forced back into exile in 1716.

George I stood back from Parliament affairs and Robert Walpole effectively governed the country between 1721 and 1742. This was a peaceful time in political terms.

Under the reign of George II, England declared war on Spain in 1739. In 1745 Charles Edward Stuart (Bonnie Prince Charlie), the son of James Edward Stuart, invaded the country in the Jacobite uprising of 1745. This uprising had less momentum than the previous one as the Hanoverians were well established and the Lowlands were generally loyalist. Twenty thousand Highland clansmen marched with Charles Edward Stuart and won the Battle of Prestonpans over the government troops. They then advanced into England and reached Derby. By December the Jacobites were threatened by the superior English forces and retreated to Scotland.

The Duke of Cumberland pursued the Jacobites and the two armies met at the Battle of Culloden in April 1746. The Jacobites were outnumbered by and had less fire power than the army of the Duke of Cumberland, and 1,200 men were killed. Many of the surviving Jacobites were slaughtered after the battle—this atrocity earned Cumberland the name 'Butcher'. Culloden ended the Jacobite rebellion and Charles went into exile for the rest of his life. The government imposed a ban on the wearing of tartan, the bearing of arms and the playing of bagpipes after Culloden and took the land of the rebel chiefs.

The private armies of the chiefs were also prohibited and the clan system was effectively destroyed.

The Highland Clearances—the removal by force of tenants and peasants to create more room for sheep—accelerated after 1815. The Highlanders experienced famine, and many left for America, leaving the Highlands largely uninhabited.

In 1760 George III, the first native English Hanoverian, became king. Under his reign Nelson interrupted Napoleon's progress at Trafalgar in 1805 and Wellington halted it at Waterloo in 1815.

The Industrial Revolution saw a move to a manufacturing economy in Britain, and Britain became financially strong. Water power was replaced by the utilization of coal as an engine fuel. In 1830 the railway age was heralded by the opening of the Liverpool-Manchester line in 1830. There was social unrest, though, and calls for parliamentary reform that resulted in the Peterloo Massacre.

George IV succeeded George III in 1820. Under his reign religious tolerance was achieved and Catholics and Nonconformists were allowed to enter parliament, workers' associations were made legal and the civilian police force was created. In 1832, under the reign of William IV, the Reform Act was passed and the system of popular representation was acknowledged.

In 1837 William IV was succeeded by his niece, Victoria. The Victorian Age saw Britain as a significant imperial power founded on industrial and commercial strength. In 1867 trade unions were fully legalized and the Irish Land Act was passed.

In 1899 Britain was in conflict with the Dutch during the Boer War. In 1914 the First World War began and the Second War World broke out in 1939.

A

Abbey Cwmhir (near Llandrindod Wells, *Powys*)

This abbey was founded in 1146 by Cistercian monks. It was designed to be one of the biggest churches in Britain. The 74-metre (242-foot) nave has only ever been exceeded in length by those of Durham, York and Winchester cathedrals. The construction of the building came to an upbrupt end in 1231 when it was destroyed by the troops of Henry III.

Aberconwy House (Conwy, *Conwy*)

This medieval merchant's house, dating from the 14th century, is the only one to have survived six centuries of Conwy's turbulent history.

Abbotsbury Abbey Remains (Abbotsbury, *Dorset*)

At this site it is possible to see the remains of the cloister of this Benedictine abbey, which was founded in 1044.

Aberdour Castle (Aberdour, *Fife*)

A 14th-century fortified tower with splendid views across the Firth of Forth. The tower, although originally built in the 14th century, was extended in the 15th, 16th and 17th centuries. Today it is possible to see remains of the residential accommodation, a bowling green, a terraced garden and a dovecote.

Aberffraw (Aberffraw, *Anglesey*)

From AD 870 until the 13th century this was the capital of North Wales.

Abergavenny Castle (Abergavenny, *Monmouthshire*)

The castle walls, towers and gateway can all still be seen at this site.

Aberlemno Sculptured Stones (Aberlemno, *Angus*)

Three carved Pictish stones dating from the 7th century line the roadside of the small village of Aberlemno. In the village churchyard there is a further stone carved with a Celtic cross and animal decorations. On the reverse of this stone a battle scene is depicted.

Abernethy Round Tower (Abernethy, *Perth and Kinross*)

The 22.5-metre (74-foot) tower dominates the village of Abernethy, which was once the royal capital of the Picts. A 7th-century carved stone can be found at the bottom of the tower.

Aberystwyth Castle (Aberystwth, *Ceredigion*)

The ruins of Edward I's 13th-century castle can seen in this town.

Abingdon County Hall (Abingdon, *Oxfordshire*)

This 17th-century public building was built to house the assize courts and is the grand centrepiece for the market place at Abingdon.

Abinger Manor (Abinger Common, *Surrey*)

At this site a small shelter covers the remains of a pi-dwelling that was occupied about 4000 years BC. It is thought that this could be the oldest man-made dwelling in Britain.

Achnabreck Cup and Ring Marks (near Lochgilphead, *Argyll and Bute*)

Cup and ring marks dating from the Bronze Age are clearly seen on this rocky ridge.

Ackling Dyke (near Salisbury, *Wiltshire*)

This is one of the finest stretches of Roman road that can be seen in Britain. It leads across 8 miles (13 kilometres) of downland to an Iron Age hillfort, Badbury Rings.

Acton Burnell Castle (Acton Burnell, *Shropshire*)

This 13th-century fortified manor house, although now ruined, was built by Robert Burnell, the Chancellor of the time.

The castle consisted of a central block with corner towers and a chapel and great hall on the first floor. The castle fell into disuse by 1420.

Addinston and Longcroft Hill Forts (near Lauderdale, *Scottish Borders*)

A hillfort built around 2700 years ago to protect a nearby settlement can be found at Addinston. Another hillfort of similar age can be found 1 mile (1.6 kilometres) away at Longcroft.

Agricola Tower *see* CHESTER CASTLE AGRICOLA TOWER.

Airds Moss (near Cumnock, *East Ayrshire*)

The stone monument here marks the site of a battle between the Covanters and the government troops in 1680. The leader of the Covanters, Richard Cameron, was killed in the battle.

A la Ronde (Summer Lane, Exmouth, *Devon*)

On their return from a tour of Europe, two cousins, Jane and Mary Parminter, instructed the building of this unique sixteen-sided house. The building was completed in 1796.

Albert Memorial (Kensington, London)

This elaborate monument was built in the early 1870s by George Gilbert Scott to commemorate the Prince Consort, husband of Queen Victoria. The 4.25-metre (14-foot) bronze figure of the Prince sits on a pyramid of 868 brick arches and is underneath a Gothic canopy that is supported by granite columns.

Albert Memorial Chapel (Windsor Castle, *Berkshire*)

This chapel was built by Henry VII but was later converted by Queen Victoria as a memorial to her husband, who died in 1861. Inside the chapel there is a monument of the Prince Consort dressed in full armour.

Aldborough Roman Town (near Boroughbridge, *North Yorkshire*)

This was the principal town of the Brigantes, the largest indigenous tribe inhabiting Roman Britain. At this site it is possible to see remains of the Roman defences and two mosaic pavements.

Alfriston Clergy House (The Tye, Alfriston, Polegate, *East Sussex*)

This 14th-century Wealden hall house is half-timbered and thatched. It contains a medieval hall and exhibition room, and its charming gardens are filled with traditional plants, some dating from Roman times. This was the first property that the National Trust acquired in 1896.

All Hallow's Barking by the Tower (Broadgate, London)

This church, although rebuilt in 1958 after being damaged in World War II, still retains an Anglo-Saxon arch dating from AD 675.

All Saints, North Street (York, *North Yorkshire*)

The most notable feature of this church is the 'Prykke of Conscience', a stained glass window of the 15th century, which depicts the last fifteen days of the world according to an Engliish mystic.

All Saints, Pavement (York, *North Yorkshire*)

The west tower of this mainly 15th-century church was rebuilt in 1800. The octagaonal lantern was introduced as a guide for travellers.

Alvecote Priory (near Tamworth, *Staffordshire*)

This ruined Benedictine priory can be found on the banks of Coventry Canal.

Ambleside Roman Fort (Ambleside, *Cumbria*)

Built to guard the Roman road from Brougham to Ravenglass, this fort is thought to date from the 1st or 2nd century.

Ancrum Moor (Lauderale, *Scottish Borders*)

This site marks a battle between the Scots and the English in 1545.

Anglesey Abbey (Lode, *Cambridgeshire*)

This Tudor manor house, which dates from 1600, was built on the site of 12th-century Augustinian abbey ruins.

Antonine Wall (central Scotland)

In AD 142 the Antonine Wall was built by the Romans between the Forth and Clyde rivers. The wall was made up of road, ditch and turf ramparts and was interspersed by forts at 2-mile (3-kilometre) intervals. One of the best-preserved forts, ROUGH CASTLE, can be seen 3 miles (5 kilometres) west of Falkirk.

Antony (Torpoint, *Cornwall*)

This is one of Cornwall's finest early 18th-century houses. It is noted for its dovecote, also 18th-century, and its Bath Pond House, which was built in 1789. This has been the home of the Carew family for nearly 600 years.

Antrim Round Tower (Antrim, *County Antrim*)

This 10th-century round tower stands in Steeple Park, which was the site of an important 6th-century monastery. The monastery was called Aemtrobh and was abandoned in 1147. The tower stands 27 metres (90 feet) high and has an unusual cross-carved stone above the lintel. A giant two-hole 'bullaun' (hollowed stone) lies at the base of the tower. This is one of the best-preserved round towers in Ireland, but there is speculation about its intended purpose. It is thought that it may have been used as a watch-tower by the monks.

Applecross (near Camusteel, Wester Ross, *Highland*)

A monastry was built here in 672 by St Maelrubha as a sanctuary for fugitives.

Appledore (Appledore, *Kent*)

This quiet village and 13th-century port has had a turbulent past. The Royal Military Canal was built in 1804 round the rim of Romney and Walland Marshes to defend the area against Napoleon. All that remains of Horne's Palace, the manor house that was beseiged by peasants angered by the 14th-century poll tax, is a small 22-foot chapel.

Appuldurcombe House (near Ventnor, *Isle of Wight*)

Built in 1701 by Sir Robert Worsley, this 18th-century baroque-style house was once the finest on the island. Today it is just a shell but it retains its elegant east front and the ornamental garden grounds that were designed by Capability Brown.

Arbor Low Stone Circle and Gib Hill Barrow (near Buxton, *Derbyshire*)

This 'STONEHENGE of Derby' consists of a flattened Stone Age circle of many massive slabs of limestone, which is surrounded by an unsually large ditch with a 76- metre (250-foot) bank. The circle is thought to be 4000 years old, and there are Bronze Age burial mounds near the site.

Arbory Hill (near Crawford, *South Lanarkshire*)

On the east bank of the Clyde on top of the hill lie the remains of a very well-preserved Iron Age fort.

Arbroath Abbey (Arbroath, *Angus*)

The abbey was founded in 1178 by King William the Lion (who is buried beneath the altar) in dedication to Thomas Becket. Today the abbey is roofless but its red sandstone walls remain. In 1320 the Declaration of Arbroath was signed at the abbey, asserting Scotland's independence: 'For so long as a hundred of us remain alive we shall never accept subjection to the domination of the English. For we fight not for glory, or riches or honour, but for freedom alone, which no good man will consent to lose but with his life.'

Ardboe Cross (Ardboe, *County Tyrone*)

This is the best example of a high cross in Northern Ireland. It marks the site of an ancient monastery and has 22 sculptured panels, which are mainly Biblical representations. The cross stands 5 metres (18 feet) high and dates back to the 10th century. The men of the village hand down the honoured tradition of 'cross reading' or interpreting the pictures on the cross.

Ardchattan Priory (near Oban, *Argyll and Bute*)
This is the ruins of a Valliscuilian priory founded in the 13th century and destroyed by Oliver Cromwell's army in 1654.

Ardestie Earth House (near Dundee, *Angus*)
A well-preserved earth house for first and second century Picts. It is 24 metres (80 feet) in length, has passages and chambers and was originally attached to a surface dwelling.

Ardlach Bell Tower (near Nairn, *Highland*)
A fortified bell tower built in 1655 that overlooks the parish church of Ardlach.

Ardontorish Castle (near Lochaline, *Argyll and Bute*)
Built in 1340, this castle was once the seat of the Lord of the Isles but now just ruins remain.

Ardress House (near Portadown, *County Armagh*)
When originally built in the 17th century, this was a rather plain house. It was transformed in 1770 by George Ensor, who added elegant wings and Adamesque plasterwork.

Ardvrech Castle (Loch Assynt, *Highland*)
This three-storey tower was built in 1597 for the Macleods of Assynt. In 1650 the Marquis of Montrose fled here for safety but was betrayed, captured and taken to Edinburgh for execution.

Argory, The (Moy, *County Armagh*)
This 19th-century Regency house has remained almost completely unaltered since the turn of the century and is full of a wide variety of treasures. It is noted for its unusual acetylene lighting system, which was installed in 1906.

Ardunie Roman Signal Station (near Auchterarder, *Perth and Kinross*)
One of a series of forts that linked Ardoch and the River Tay, dating back to the 1st century.

Argyll Lodging (Stirling, *Stirling*)

A well-preserved town house built in the 16th century and extended by the Earl of Argyll in 1674. It was used as a military hospital between 1800 and 1950.

Arisaig (Arisaig, *Highland*)

This village was used as a base by Bonnie Prince Charlie during the 1745 Jacobite uprising.

Armagh Friary (Armagh, *County Armagh*)

The remains of the longest friary church in Ireland, 49 metres (163 feet), can be found inside the gates of the former Archbishop's Palace. The friary was founded in 1263 by Archbishop O'Scanaail but was destoyed by Shane O'Neill in the mid-16th century. It was destroyed to prevent it being garrisoned by Elizabethan soldiers.

Arnol Black House (Arnol, Lewis, *Western Isles*)

A traditional black house on Lewis. It has walls that are 1.8 metres (6 feet) thick and a thatched roof tied down and weighted with stones.

Arthur's Round Table (Eamont Bridge, *Cumbria*)

This prehistoric circular earthwork is bounded by a ditch and an outer bank.

Arthur's Stone (Dorstone, *Hereford and Worcester*)

This impressive prehistoric burial chamber is formed by large blocks of stone.

Arundel (Arundel, *West Sussex*)

This famous castle was built in the period following the Norman conquest to defend the Arun valley, one of the six Sussex regions in Norman times. It is the ancestral home of the Dukes of Norfolk.

Ashby de la Zouch Castle (Ashby de la Zouch, *Leicestershire*)

The ruins of this outstanding late-medieval castle are dominated by the splendid 24-metre (80-foot) Hastings Tower, dating from the 15th century, which was split in two during the Civil War. Henry VIII, Mary Queen of Scots, James I and VI and Charles I were all entertained at this castle.

Ashdown House (Lambourn, *Berkshire*)

This tower-like, four storey house was built by the first Lord Craven around 1660 and was 'consecrated' to Elizabeth, Queen of Bohemia. It has an enormous staircase from ground to roof and boasts wide views over the downs.

Ashleworth Tithe Barn (Ashleworth, *Gloucestershire*)

This 15th-century tithe barn has two porch bays and fine roof timbers with queenposts.

Ashmolean Museum (Oxford, *Oxfordshire*)

This is Britain's oldest public museum and was opened in 1683. It is still open today and has a fine collection of paintings and relics.

Aston Hall (near Birmingham, West Midlands)

This was one of the last, great Jacobean houses to be built in England and was completed in 1635. It is a splendid sight with its gables, arches, domes and octagonal chimneys, and is noted for its 41-metre (135-foot) Long Gallery, which has arcaded oak panelling.

Attingham Park (Shrewsbury, *Shropshire*)

This elegant, late 18th-century Neoclassical mansion has splendid state rooms and was built for the first Lord Berwick. The central portico, with 12-metre (40-foot) columns, rises three storeys.

Auchagallon Stone Circle (near Blackwaterfoot, Arran, *North Ayrshire*)

A Bronze Age burial cairn with fifteen standing stones surrounding it.

Auckland Castle Deer House (Bishop Auckland, *County Durham*)

This charming mid-18th-century building was erected in the

park of the bishops of Durham so that deer could find shelter and food.

Audley End (near Saffron Walden, *Essex*)

When it was built by the first Earl of Suffolk, Lord Treasurer to James I, Audley End was considered to be one of the great wonders of the nation. The great Jacobean mansion, one of the most significant in England, was built on the scale of a royal palace and became just that when Charles I bought it in 1668. The house has been much altered since it was first constructed and today is much reduced in size.

Audley's Castle (Strangford, *County Down*)

This 15th-century tower house has complete internal fittings.

Australian Settlers' Monument (Portsmouth, *Hampshire*)

This chain-link sculpture was errected to commemorate the first convict ships that set sail for Australia in 1787.

Avebury Stone Circle (Avebury, *Wiltshire*)

This is one of Britain's most impressive prehistoric sites with its complex, huge and mysterious stone circles. The circles were constructed 4000 years ago and originally consisted of in excess of 180 stones. At the site it is possible to see two stone circles surrounded by an outer circle, which is the largest in Europe. The larger circle is in turn surrounded by a henge, which consists of a ditch and a large bank. Originally, the bank stood 16.75 metres (55 feet) high, and it was made of brilliant white chalk. At the southern entrance there is evidence of a stone avenue that is thought to have been used for processions.'

Aydon Castle (near Corbridge, *Northumberland*)

This is one of the most splendid fortified manor houses in England. It was built in the late 13th century but was converted into a farmhouse in the 17th century. The most notable feature is the Great Hall.

Ayton Castle (near Scarborough, *North Yorkshire*)
At this site lie the remains of a fortified medieval tower that was built in the style of a Scottish peel tower and served as both a house and a fortress. Today all that can be seen is the base of the tower.

B

Baconsthorpe Castle (near Baconsthorpe, *Norfolk*)
At this site it is possible to see the remains of the gatehouses of a ruined 15th-century fortified manor house that was partly surrounded by a moat.

Badbury Rings *see* ACKLING DYKE.

Baddlesey Clinton (Lapworth, *Warwickshire*)
This medieval moated manor houses dates from the 14th century and has undergone little change since 1634.

Baguley Hall (Baguley, *Greater Manchester*)
This medieval hall house dates from the 14th century and has had additions in the 18th and 19th centuries.

Balliol College (Oxford, *Oxfordshire*)
John de Baliol planned this building as a penance after he had insulted the Bishop of Durham. A fire that put Bishops Latimer and Ridley to their deaths charred the doors in the corner of the Front Quad.

Ballowall Barrow (St Just, *Cornwall*)
With its complex layout, this is an unusual example of a Bronze Age chambered tomb.

Ballycopeland Windmill (Donaghadee, *County Down*)
This is the only complete, working windmill in Northern Ireland. It was built in the late 18th century and was in use until 1914. It was used to mill wheat and oats and to make animal

feed. The windmill is noted for its intricate wooden machinery.

Ballygowan Cup and Ring Marks (near Kilmartin, *Argyll and Bute*)
Bronze Age cup and ring marks on natural rock faces can be seen here.

Ballymoney Heritage Farm Park (Ballymoney, *County Antrim*)
This 18th-century estate has a Georgian house and period farm buildings.

Ballyumford Dolmen (Ballyumford, *County Antrim*)
The remains of this 4–5000-year-old single-chamber Neolithic tomb, known as the Druid's Altar, can be found in the front garden of a house on Ballyumford Road.

Balmerino Abbey (Balmerino, *Fife*)
Balmerino Abbey was a Cisterian monastery founded by Alexander II and his mother, Queen Ermynagarde, who is buried beneath the high altar. The ruins can be seen on the hilltop as well as a 450-year-old Spanish chestnut tree planted in the grounds.

Baluachraig Cup and Ring Marks (near Kilmartin, *Argyll and Bute*)
Several groups of Bronze Age cup and ring marks on natural rock are seen at this site.

Balvaird Castle (near Bridge of Earn, *Perth and Kinross*)
This is an L-shaped 15th-century tower house that was extended in 1581 to include a walled courtyard and gatehouse.

Balvenie Castle (Dufftown, *Moray*)
This 13th-century ruined castle was the site at which the victorous Jacobite troops gathered after the Battle of Killiecrankie. The castle is noted for its defensive structure with its high stone walls and double iron gates.

Banagher Church (Dungiven, *County Londonderry*)
This church was founded at the start of the 12th century by St Muiredach O'Heney and was altered in later centuries. The re-

mains that can be seen today are impressive and include the
nave and the square-headed lintelled west door. Outside there
is a well-preserved minature house that is thought to be the
tomb of St Muiredach.

Banks East Turret (near Banks, *Cumbria*)

This well-preserved turret adjoins stretches of HADRIAN'S
WALL.

Bannockburn (Stirling, *Stirling*)

This is one of the most important historic sites in Scotland. In
June 1314 the Scots, led by their king, Robert the Bruce, defeated the English, led by Edward II, in the battle here, win-
ning independence for the Scottish people and ending English
domination.

Banqueting House (Whitehall, London)

This hall, built in the classical style, survives from Whitehall
Palace, which was designed by Indigo Jones in 1619. In 1635
Charles I commisioned Peter Paul Rubens to paint the ceiling
of the chamber.

**Bant's Carn Burial Chamber and Halangy Down Ancient
Village** (St Mary's, *Isles of Scilly*)

This Bronze Age burial mound has an entrance passage and
chamber and lies above the site of an ancient Iron Age village.

Barbury Castle (near Swindon, *Wiltshire*)

This is an Iron Age hillfort with two ditches and a rampart, and
it covers some 12 acres. It stands on the Ridgeway, which was
a prehistoric track running from South Devon to the Wash.

Bardsey Island (near Aberdaron, *Gwynedd*)

This is said to be the burial place of many holy men and of
Merlin, King Arthur's wizard.

Barnard Castle (Barnard Castle, *County Durham*)

Overlooking the River Tees, this large castle has substantial
parts that remain intact. Today it is still possible to see parts of

the 14th-century Great Hall and the cylindrical 12th-century tower.

Barochan Cross (Paisley Abbey, Paisley, *Renfrewshire*)
A free-standing Celtic cross stands at Paisley Abbey in the centre of Paisley.

Barrow Cemetery *see* BOW HILL.

Barsalloch Fort (*Dumfries and Galloway*)
This is an Iron Age hillfort defended by a deep ditch.

Basing House (near Basingstoke, *Hampshire*)
This was once the largest private house in Tudor England. It was destroyed by Cromwell's troops during a siege in 1645.

Basingwerk Abbey (Greenfield Valley Heritage Park, *Flintshire*)
This ruined abbey was founded in 1132 by Cistercian monks.

Bath Abbey (Bath, *Bath and North East Somerset*)
The abbey is built in Perpendicular Gothic style and has a 49-metre (162-foot) tower, flying buttresses and fan vaulting. The building of the abbey began in 1499 on the site of the original abbey, which was founded by the local king, Osric, in about AD 680.

Bath Assembly Rooms (Bath, *Bath and North East Somerset*)
This is one of Bath's finest public buildings and was at one time considered the grandest in Europe. It was built 1769–71 by the architect John Wood the Younger for social activities.

Bath Pond House *see* ANTONY.

Battle Abbey and Battlefield (Battle, *East Sussex*)
The date of the Battle of Hastings, 1066, is probably the most memorable date in English history. It was at this battle on 14 October that the conquering Normans vanquished the Anglo-Saxons. The armies did not in fact fight at Hastings but on the site of what was later to become Battle, some 6 miles (10 kilo-metres) inland. King William built an abbey to atone for the blood spilt at the battle, and in the ruins of the abbey it is pos-

sible to stand on the spot where King Harold finally fell.

Bayard's Cove Fort (Dartmouth, *Devon*)

This small artillery fort was built some time prior to 1534 to defend the entrance to Dartmouth harbour.

Bayham Old Abbey (near Lamberhurst, *Kent*)

At this site there are the ruins of a house of 'white' canons, which was founded in the early 13th century.

Beaghmore Stone Circles and Alignments (Beaghmore, *County Tyrone*)

These ritualistic stones are thought to date back to the Neolithic or Bronze Age. There are three pairs of stone circles, one single stone circle, stone rows and cairns. Many historic monuments have been discovered in this area.

Beauly Priory (Beauly, *Highland*)

One of three Vallisculian priories founded in 1230. The ruins of the church remain today and contain a 16th-century monument to Kenneth Mackenzie.

Beaumaris Castle (Beaumaris, *Anglesey*)

This was the last Welsh fortification to be built by Edward I. It took from 1295 to 1312 to complete and involved a massive number of workmen. A document of 1296 mentions 400 masons and 2000 labourers. It was captured by Owain Glyndwr in the early 15th century. It was retaken later and in following centuries it was looted for lead, timber and stone. It still remains one of the best-preserved castles built by Edward I. Two incomplete gatehouses can also be seen. The outer curtain wall and small towers also survive.

Beaumaris Courthouse (Beaumaris, *Anglesey*)

This is the oldest active courthouse in Britain. It was built in 1614.

Beaumaris Gaol (Beaumaris, *Anglesey*)

Here it is possible to see evidence of the tough penalties exacted in the 19th century. The route that condemned prisoners took to the scaffold can still be seen.

Beaupre Castle *see* OLD BEAUPRE CASTLE.

Bede's World Museum *see* ST PAUL'S MONASTERY.

Beeston Castle (near Chester, *Cheshire*)
The ruins of the castle lie on top of Beeston Hill. A party of Royalists held out here for six months following the defeat of Charles I in 1645.

Belas Knap Long Barrow (near Winchcombe, *Gloucestershire*)
This a good example of a Neolithic long barrow. The mound is still intact and is surrounded by a stone wall. The chamber tombs have been opened up, and the remains of over 30 people were found inside.

Belfast Castle (Belfast)
This great Scottish baronial style castle was built in 1870 by the third Marquis of Donegal. It has a great square six-storey tower and a baroque staircase. In 1934 it was presented to the city of Belfast by the Earl of Shaftesbury and restored in 1980.

Belleek Pottery (Belleek, *County Fermanagh*)
This is Ireland's oldest and most historic pottery and is famed for the production of fine Parian china. It was started in 1857 by the Caldwell family, who originally used feldspar from the Castle Caldwell estate.

Benburb Castle (Benburb, *County Tyrone*)
This castle was built in 1615. The remains include three towers and the massive walls.

Beningbrough Hall (near Shipton, *North Yorkshire*)
This impressive Georgian hall was built in 1716 and contains exquisite carvings and a cantilevered staircase.

Benwell Roman Temple (Newcastle upon Tyne, *Tyne and Wear*)
The remains of this small temple at HADRIAN'S WALL are surrounded by modern housing.

Benwell Vallum Crossing (Newcastle upon Tyne, *Tyne and Wear*)

This is the sole remaining example of an original stone-built causeway across the ditch of the vallum earthwork that ran parallel to HADRIAN'S WALL.

Berkeley Castle (Berkeley, *Gloucestershire*)

This medieval fortress has been the home of the Berkeley family for more than 800 years. The castle has a cell where Edward II was brutally murdered in 1327. The ramparts of the castle were damaged by Cromwell's troops during the Civil Wall—breaches in the wall can still be seen.

Berkhamsted Castle (Berkhamstead, *Hertfordshire*)

The extensive remains of a large 11th-century motte-and-bailey castle can be seen at this site.

Berry Pomreroy Castle (near Totnes, *Devon*)

This romantic late-medieval castle is unusual as it combines the remains of a large castle with a courtier's mansion.

Berwick-upon-Tweed Castle (Berwick-upon-Tweed, *Northumberland*)

This 12th-century castle is now in ruins.

Berwick-upon-Tweed Ramparts (Berwick-upon-Tweed, *Northumberland*)

Measuring some 1½ miles (2.4 kilometres) long, 6 metres (20 feet) high and incredibly thick, these ramparts are still in pristine condition. Elizabeth I invested vast amounts of money in the defences of Berwick-upon-Tweed fearing a French or Scottish invasion. Neither the Scots nor the French did attack and so Berwick was left with rather unnecessarily elaborate defences.

Berwick-upon-Tweed Barracks (Berwick-upon-Tweed, *Northumberland*)

Built in 1717, these are among the earliest purpose-built barracks and they have been left much unchanged.

Bicknoller Hill (near Bridgwater Bay, *Somerset*)
On the southern slopes of this hill lie the remains of the Iron Age settlement, Trendle Ring.

Biggar Gasworks (Biggar, *South Lanarkshire*)
Dating from 1839, Biggar has the only surviving coal-gas works in Scotland, now under the care of Historic Scotland.

Bignor (Bignor, *West Sussex*)
This village boasts a large Roman villa with fine mosaics. The Roman Stane Street runs nearby and on Bignor Hill, 1¼ miles (2 kilometres) to the south, is the site of a large Stone Age enclosure, one of the largest camps with a causeway in Britain.

Binchester Fort (near Bishop Auckland, *County Durham*)
This Roman cavalry fort has well-preserved hypocausts. The concrete floor is still intact in one of the rooms and is supported on brick piers.

Binham Priory (near Binham-on-Wells, *Norfolk*)
At this site it is possible to see the extensive remains of a Benedictine priory. The original nave of the church is still used as the parish church.

Birdoswald Fort (near Greenhead, *Northumberland*)
At this site on HADRIAN'S WALL it is possible to see evidence of the fort's granaries, west gate and east gate, which is amongst the best-preserved on the Wall.

Birnham Wayside Cross (Birnham, *Norfolk*)
This medieval cross marks the site of an annual fair that was held here from the reign of Henry I until the 1950s.

Birsay, Brough of *see* BROUGH OF BIRSAY.

Bishop's and Earl's Palaces (Kirkwall, *Orkney*)
The Bishop's Palace is a 12th-century hall-house that was altered by the addition of a round tower built by Bishop Reid in the 1540s. The adjacent Earl's Palace was built by the Earl of Orkney, Patrick Stewart, in 1677 in Renaissance style.

Bishop's Waltham Palace (Bishop's Waltham, *Hampshire*)

At this site it is possible to see the 12th and 14th-century remains of the medieval seat of the Bishops of Winchester. Of notable interest are the Great Hall, the moat and three-storey tower. The palace was largely destroyed in a fire set by Parliamentarians during the Civil War following the Battle of Cheriton in 1644.

Black Carts Turret (near Chollerton, *Northumberland*)

This 457-metre (500-yard) length of HADRIAN'S WALL has turret foundations.

Black Down (near Dorchester, *Dorset*)

A hill-top obelisk commemmorates Sir Thomas Masterman Hardy, the captain of Nelson's flagship, HMS *Victory*, at the Battle of Trafalgar in 1805.

Blackbury Camp (near Southleigh, *Devon*)

At this site there is an Iron Age hillfort that is defended by a bank and a ditch.

Blackfriars (Gloucester, *Gloucestershire*)

Most of this small 13th-century Dominican priory church remains intact. It is noted for its unusual scissor-braced roof.

Blackfriars Chapel (St Andrews, *Fife*)

A vaulted apse remains of this church of Dominican friars. It was rebult in 1516.

Blackhall Roman Camps (Ardoch, *Perth and Kinross*)

Here there are the remains of the defensive structure of two Roman camps dating from the early 3rd century.

Blackhammer Chambered Cairn (Rousay, *Orkney*)

This is a Neolithic chambered cairn with retaining wall. The chamber is divided into seven compartments.

Blackhill (*South Lanarkshire*)

An Iron Age fort and a bronze can be found on top of Blackhill, which has wonderful views over the Clyde valley.

Black House *see* ARNOL BLACK HOUSE.

Blackness Castle (near Linlithgow, *West Lothian*)

This castle of the 1440s was strengthened in the 1500s to be used as an artillery fortress and latterly in the 1870s as an ammunition depot. Its picturesque courtyard has been used as a setting in several films.

Blaenavon Ironworks (near Pontypool, *Torfaen*)

The substantial remains of five early blast furnaces dating from 1788 can be seen at this site. Remains of workers' housing can also be seen.

Blood Rock *see* DUNAVERTY ROCK.

Bluebottle Grove *see* LEXDEN EARTHWORKS.

Boarstall Tower (Boarstall, *Buckinghamshire*)

Dating from the 14th century, this stone gatehouse is all that remains of a fortified house. It was altered in the 16th and 17th centuries but retains its crossloops for bows.

Bodiam Castle (Bodiam, *East Sussex*)

This was built in 1385 as a defence against an anticipated French invasion that never came. It was also used as a comfortable dwelling place for rich nobles. The exterior of the castle is almost complete, and the battlements and spiral staircases also remain.

Bolingbroke Castle (Old Bolingbroke, *Lincolnshire*)

This 13th-century castle was the birthplace of Henry IV in 1367. It was later beseiged by Parliamentary forces in 1643.

Bolsover Castle (Bolsover, *Derbyshire*)

This is an early 17th-century mansion that was built on the site of a Norman castle. With its hill-top setting it dominates the surrounding countryside.

Bolton Abbey (near Skipton, *North Yorkshire*)

The ruins of this charming 12th-century Augustinian priory can be seen amongst woods, meadows and waterfalls.

Bonamargy Friary (Ballycastle, *County Antrim*)

This was founded at the start of the 16th century by Rory MacQuillan and was later passed on to the MacDonnels, Earls of Antrim. Today, remains of the friary's gatehouse, church and cloister can still be seen.

Bonawe Iron Works (near Taynuilt, *Argyll and Bute*)

Founded in 1753, this is the most impressive and complete iron works in Britain to be fuelled by charcoal.

Bootham Bar (York, *North Yorkshire*)

This 14th-century gateway has two hanging turrets.

Borth-y-Gest (Borth-y-Gest, *Gwynedd*)

Legend tells that Prince Madog sailed from here to discover America. His journey is said to have been undertaken 300 years prior to that of Christopher Columbus.

Boscabel House (near Wolverley, *Shropshire*)

This 17th-century timber-framed hunting lodge was used as a hiding place by King Charles II after the Battle of Worcester in 1651. He hid here and in the Royal Oak to avoid detection by Cromwell's troops.

Bosherston (Bosherston, *Pembrokeshire*)

Local legend tells that King Arthur disposed of Excalibur here when he was dying.

Bosworth Field (near Sutton Cheney, *Leicestershire*)

This is the site where, in 1485, Richard III fell to the forces of Henry Tudor, the future Henry VII. The flags of the two opposing armies still fly here to this day.

Bothwell Castle (Uddingston, *South Lanarkshire*)

This 13th-century stone castle was extended in the 14th and 15th centuries to become the largest in Scotland. Today part of the original keep remains. This castle was the scene of many a bloody battle during the Wars of Indepedence between Scotland and England.

Bourne (Bourne, *Lincolnshire*)

This was the home town of local hero Hereward the Wake, the last Saxon noble to resist William the Conquerer.

Bow Bridge (Barrow-in-Furness, *Cumbria*)

This late medieval stone bridge was built across Mill Beck, carrying a route to FURNESS ABBEY.

Bow Hill (near Singleton, *West Sussex*)

The Bronze Age sites here, at Barrow Cemetery, are among the best-preserved in the country.

Bowes Castle (Bowes, *County Durham*)

These massive ruins of Henry II's tower keep stand three storeys high and are set within the earthworks of a Roman fort.

Boxgrove Priory (near Boxgrove, *West Sussex*)

At this site lie the remains of the guest house, chapterhouse and church of a 12th-century priory.

Bradford-on-Avon Tithe Barn (Bradford-on-Avon, *Wiltshire*)

This medieval stone-built barn has a slate roof and wooden beamed interior.

Brading Roman Villa (near Sandown, *Isle of Wight*)

This 3rd-century AD villa was the centre of a Roman agricultural estate. The remains include splendid mosaic floors, some of which have underfloor heating.

Bramber Castle (Bramber, *West Sussex*)

The castle gatehouse, walls and earthworks of this Norman castle ruin can be seen at this site.

Brandsbutt Symbol Stone (Inverurie, *Aberdeenshire*)

This is a carved Pictish symbol stone with an ogam inscription.

Bratton Castle (near Westbury, *Wiltshire*)

At this site there lies a large double-walled Iron Age hillfort that covers 25 acres on Westbury Hill. There is also a white horse that was carved into the chalk of the hillside in 1778.

Brechin Cathedral Round Tower (Brechin, *Angus*)

This is an 11th-century round tower of the Irish style with a splendid carved entance and a stone roof added in the 1400s.

Brecon Castle (Brecon, *Powys*)

The tower and a battlemented section of wall remain of this castle built by Bernard Newmarch, half-brother of William the Conqueror.

Brecon Cathedral (Brecon, *Powys*)

The north and south walls of the nave and the 12th-century font remain from the Norman period of this cathedral.

Bridestones (near Macclesfield, *Cheshire*)

The remains of this 91-metre (300-foot) Neolithic long barrow include burial chamber, forecourt and long gallery.

Bridge of Oich (Fort Augustus, *Highland*)

The suspension bridge here was designed by James Dredge in 1850.

Brinkburn Priory (near Rothbury, *Northumberland*)

A fine example of early Gothic architecture, this late 12th-century church is almost perfectly preserved.

Bristol Cathedral (City of Bristol)

This was originally founded in 1140 as the Abbey Church of St Augustine on the legendary site where St Augustine met early Christians in the 7th century. It is noted for its Norman chapterhouse, 14th-century choir and ruined nave.

British Camp *see* HEREFORDSHIRE BEACON.

Broadaun Ring (Postbridge, *Devon*)

This prehistoric walled pound encloses a group of hut circles, thought to have been used to pen sheep and cattle.

Broch of Gurness (near Kirkwall, *Orkney*)

In a beautiful setting looking across to the islands of Rousay and Wyre, this is a circular drystone tower surrounded by ditches and ramparts and a warren of Iron Age buildings.

Brocolita (Newbrough, *Northumberland*)

This Roman fort on HADRIAN'S WALL has a temple of Mithras, the Persian god of light.

Brodick Castle (Brodick, Isle of Arran, *North Ayrshire*)

The site of Brodick Castle has been a fortress since Viking times. The castle that exists today dates from the 13th century with extensions in 1652 and 1844.

Brodie Castle (*Moray*)

Built in the 16th century for the Brodie family and extended in the 17th and 19th centuries, the castle suffered some damage during the Montrose campaigns in 1645.

Brodsworth Hall (Brodsworth, *South Yorkshire*)

This is one of England's most beautiful Victorian country houses. It has remained almost intact since the 1860s.

Bronllys Castle (Bronllys, *Powys*)

This castle was built in the 13th century in an attempt to control the troubled borders.

Brough Castle (near Appleby, *Cumbria*)

On a site important since Roman times, Brough Castle was built in the 12th century to replace a stronghold destroyed by the Scots in 1174.

Brough of Birsay (near Kirkwall, *Orkney*)

This tidal island off the coast of Orkney at Birsay marks the spot of a ruined Norse village and church.

Brougham Castle (near Penrith, *Cumbria*)

The impressive ruins of this castle include an early 13th-century keep and some later buildings. There is also an exhibition of Roman tombstones taken from a nearby fort.

Broughty Castle (Broughty Ferry, *Angus*)

A 16th-century tower, adapted in 1860, which is perched on a rocky outcrop above the harbour.

Brown Caterthun *see* CATERTHUNS.

Bruce's Stone (*Dumfries and Galloway*)

A granite boulder on Moss Raploch marks the site where King Robert the Bruce led the Scots to defeat the English in battle in 1307.

Brunton Turret (near Low Brunton, *Northumberland*)

This 64-metre (70-yard) stretch of HADRIAN'S WALL has a well-preserved 2.4-metre (8-foot) high turret.

Bryn-Celli-Ddu Burial Chamber (Bryncelli Ddu, *Anglesey*)

This Stone Age burial mound is thought to be 4000 years old. A passage leads to the 3-metre (10-foot) long central chamber, which has an upright stone that is thought to have been used to perform sacrificial rituals.

Buchan Stone *see* LOUDON WOOD STONE CIRCLE.

Buckfast Abbey (near Ashburton, *Devon*)

It took six monks 31 years to build this replica of a 12th-century Cistercian abbey. It has a magnificent altar and splendid mosaic floors.

Buckingham Palace (The Mall, London)

Now the residence of the British monarchy, the palace was rebuilt from the former Buckingham House of 1703. Rebuilding began in 1825 by John Nash for George IV. The first monarch to take up residence here was Queen Victoria in 1837.

Buckland Abbey (Yelverton, *Devon*)

This 13th-century abbey has the secrets of over 700 years of history. It has in its time been a Cistercian monastery, the home of Sir Richard Grenville and also the home of Sir Frances Drake.

Buildwas Abbey (near Ironbridge, *Shropshire*)

The extensive remains of this 12th-century Cistercian abbey lie on the banks of the River Severn.

Burgh Castle (Breydon Water, near Great Yarmouth, *Norfolk*)

The walls, with projecting bastions, are all that remain of this

Roman fort that was built in the late 3rd century as one of a chain of forts to defend the coast against Saxon invaders.

Burleigh Castle (Milnathort, *Perth and Kinross*)

This is an early 16th-century tower frequently visited by James IV.

Burry Holms (near Swansea, *Swansea*)

This small island has an Iron Age fort and the ruins of a 12th-century church that was built in dedication to St Cennyd, a 6th-century hermit.

Bury St Edmunds Abbey (Bury St Edmunds, *Suffolk*)

The Norman tower and 14th-century gatehouse are the notable remains of this Benedictine abbey, church and precinct.

Bushmead Priory (near Colmworth, *Bedfordshire*)

The medieval refectory of this Augustinian priory is largely intact. It has its original timber-framed roof and it contains wall paintings and stained glass.

Byland Abbey (near Thirsk, *North Yorkshire*)

The west front of the church of this 12th-century monastery still stands. Other remains include the layout of the monastic site.

C

Cadbury Castle (near South Cadbury, *Somerset*)

This ancient hillfort is alleged to have been the site of Camelot, the seat of King Arthur's court. The ramparts that encircle the fort date back to the Iron Age but were added to until Saxon times.

Caer Caradoc (near Shrewsbury, *Shropshire*)

The British chieftan Caractacus is said to have made his last stand against the Romans at this hillfort in AD 50.

Caerlaverock Castle (near Dumfries, *Dumfries and Galloway*)
This is a spectacular castle on a triangular site (the only one in Scotland) surrounded by moats. The entrance is guarded by a twin-towered gatehouse.

Caerleon Fortress Baths, Amphitheatre and Barracks (Caerleon, *Newport*)
Caerleon was an important Roman military base, accommodating thousands of men. Today the foundations of barrack lines and parts of the ramparts can still be seen, as can remains of the cookhouse, latrines and baths. The nearby amphitheatre is one of the best examples in Britain. The fortress baths is one of the most complete examples of a Roman legionary bath building in Britain.

Caernarfon Castle (Caernarfon, *Gwynedd*)
This castle was begun in 1283 by Edward I. It was the strongest link in his Iron Ring and was designed to supress any Welsh aspirations of autonomy and to symbolize Anglo-Norman military strength. Edward I intended this to be a royal residence and the seat of government for North Wales.

Caerphilly Castle (Caerphilly, *Caerphilly*)
This was the first castle in Britain to be built concentrically, with an inner defensive structure overlooking the outer ring. The castle was founded in 1268 by Gilbert de Clare as a defence against Llewelyn the Last. The castle was largely destroyed by Llewelyn in 1270. It was rebuilt almost immediately, but for the following centuries was allowed to deteriorate by successive kings.

Caerwent Roman Town (near Caerwent, *Monmouthshire*)
A complete circuit of the town wall of the Roman town of Venta Silurum and excavated shops, houses and temple can be seen at this site.

Caer y Twr *see* Cytiau'r Gwyddelod.

Cairn Holy Chambered Cairns (near Creetown, *Dumfries and Galloway*)

Two practically complete burial cairns dating from the Neolithic Age lie on a hill-top position overlooking Wigtown Bay.

Cairnbaan Cup and Ring Marks (Lochgilphead, *Argyll and Bute*)

Cup and ring marks cut into the natural rock face can be seen at this site.

Cairn o' Get (near Lybster, *Highland*)

A horned and chambered burial cairn can be seen at this site.

Cairnpapple Hill (near Bathgate, *West Lothian*)

An important prehistoric monument, this site was used as a burial chamber between 3000 and 1400 BC.

Caister Roman Site (near Caister-on-Sea, *Norfolk*)

The remains of a 3rd-century Roman town, including a gateway, defensive wall and buildings along a main street, can be seen at this site.

Caiy Stone (Fairmilehead, Edinburgh)

This 2.75-metre (9-foot) stone pillar marks the site of an ancient battle between the Romans and the Picts. It is also known as the Kel Stone and General Kay's monument.

Caldicot Castle (Caldicot, *Monmouthshire*)

This restored 11th-century castle has an impressive gatehouse and keep. The fortifications were founded by the Normans and fully developed by the late 14th century.

Callanish (Calanais) Standing Stones (near Stornoway, Lewis, *Western Isles*)

A cross-shaped arrangement of standing stones dating from around 3000 bc can be seen at this site. This formation of stones is unique in Scotland.

Calshot Castleb (near Fawley, *Hampshire*)

This coastal fort was built by Henry VIII to defend the sea passage to Southampton.

Camber Castle (near Rye, *East Sussex*)

The ruins of this castle built for Henry VIII survive in the original plan.

Cambuskenneth Abbey (near Stirling, *Stirling*)

Cambuskenneth Abbey was the site of Robert the Bruce's parliament in 1326. James III and his queen are buried here. Today the tower is the only significant remaining section but the majority of the foundations remain.

Camelford (Camelford, *Cornwall*)

Local legend tells that this was the site of King Arthur's Camelot. The site of the king's last battle, against Mordred, his rebellious nephew, is said to be near Slaughter Bridge.

Campbeltown (Kintyre, *Argyll and Bute*)

Campbeltown was formerly the Celtic capital of the ancient Scottish Dalriada kingdom, and the town centre has a fine carved Celtic cross.

Canongate Kirk (High Street, Edinburgh)

The construction of this 17th-century church was ordered by James II and VII for the residents of the Royal Mile and the Old Town.

Cantef-y-Gwaelod *see* WALLOG.

Canterbury Cathedral (Canterbury, *Kent*)

This is the mother church of the Church of England and the seat of the Primate of All England. There has been a cathedral here since 602. In 1070 Lanfranc, the first Norman archbishop, levelled the existing Saxon structure and built a new cathedral. Since being built it has been extensively modified and altered. One of the most stiking modifications is the Bell Harry Tower, 71.5 metres (235 feet) high, which was added in 1505. The Trinity Chapel holds the tomb of Henry IV and his wife, Joan of Navarre. There is also a gilded effigy of Edward II's son, the Black Prince. The cathedral was noted for its shrine to the martyred Thomas a Becket, which made Canterbury a place of pilgrimage. Henry VIII had the shrine destroyed in 1538.

Cantlop Bridge (near Berrington, *Shropshire*)

This single-span cast-iron road bridge over the Cound Brook was designed by Thomas Telford.

Cardiff Castle (Cardiff, *Cardiff*)

This was originally the site of a Roman fort. A neat Norman motte is topped with an 11th-century keep that overlooks the towers and turrets of the domestic buildings below, which date from the 14th century. The domestic buildings were greatly extended in Tudor times and transformed by the third Marquis of Bute in the late 19th century.

Cardoness Castle (near Gatehouse of Fleet, *Dumfries and Galloway*)

Cardoness was built in the 15th century and was the home of the McCullochs. The tower is well preserved and gives a commanding view over Fleet Bay.

Carew Castle (Carew, *Pembrokeshire*)

This magnificent 12th-century castle bult by Sir Nicholas de Carew and extended in Tudor times is now in ruins, but the stone-mullioned windows are still of note.

Carisbrooke Castle (near Newport, *Isle of Wight*)

The site of this castle has been important since a Saxon camp was founded here in the 8th century. The first connection between Carisbrooke and royalty was at the end of the 13th century when it was purchased by Edward I. It was here that Charles I was imprisoned before his execution in 1649.

Carlisle Castle (Carlisle, *Cumbria*)

For over nine centuries this castle has defended the western end of the Anglo-Scottish border. It was first built in 1092 after William II relieved Carlisle of 200 years of Scottish rule.

From that time until the union of the crowns in 1603 it was fought over constantly by the two nations. It was later won by the Scots during the Civil War and the Jacobite Rising a hundred years later.

Carlungie Earth House (near Monifieth, *Angus*)

This underground earth house dating from the Iron Age measures 45.75 metres (150 feet) in length.

Carmarthen (Carmarthen, *Carmarthenshire*)

Originally founded as a Roman fort, Carmarthen is the legendary birthplace of the wizard Merlin. Today it is possible to see the remains of a Norman castle and the site of a Roman amphitheatre.

Carnasserie Castle (Kilmartin, *Argyll and Bute*)

A fine tower house with hall, Carnasserie was the home of the first Protestant Bishop of the Isles.

Carn Baan (near Lagg, *Argyll and Bute*)

An impressive Neolithic long cairn, one of the most important in the south of Scotland.

Carne Beacon (Nare Head, near Carne, *Cornwall*)

This Bronze Age mound is the legendary burial place of a Cornish king and his ship.

Carn Euny Ancient Village (near Sancreed, *Cornwall*)

The foundations of stone huts and an interesting curved underground passage can be found at the remains of this Iron Age settlement.

Carn Liath (near Golspie, *Highland*)

Carn Liath is an example of a typical broch of the Sutherland area. The first floor remains intact, and there is an associated settlement close by.

Carreg Cennen Castle (near Trap, *Carmarthenshire*)

This was first built as a stonghold of the native Welsh. It was rebuilt in the late 13th century. The impressive remains include a mysterious passage cut into the side of the cliff and lit by loopholes.

Carreg Samson (near Abercastle, *Pembrokeshire*)

This is a Stone Age burial chamber to the west of the port.

Carrick-a-Rede Rope Bridge (Carrick-a-Rede, *County Antrim*)

Each spring for over 300 years the rope bridge has been put across the 18-metre (60-foot) gap between cliffs and a rocky island. It is then dismantled each autumn.

Carrickfergus Castle (Carrickfergus, *County Antrim*)

This is the best-preserved Norman castle in Ireland. It was built after 1180 by John de Courcy, Earl of Ulster. It was used for military purposes for over 800 years and is thought to be one of the most fought-over castles in Ireland.

Carsluith Castle (near Creetown, *Dumfries and Galloway.*)

The ruin of this 16th-century has been well preserved. Additional buildings dating from the 18th century can also be seen.

Cartmel Priory Gatehouse (Cartmel, *Cumbria*)

This gatehouse and the church are all that remain of the Augustinian priory that was founded here about 1330.

Castell Coch (near Tongwynlais, *Cardiff*)

This unique fairy-tale castle dates from the late 19th century. It was designed by William Burgess for the third Marquis of Bute. It is decorated in the Victorian Gothic style.

Castell Henllys Fort (Crymych, *Pembrokeshire*)

Three roundhouses have been reconstructed at the excavated site of this Iron Age hillfort.

Castell y Bere (near Llanegryn, *Gwynedd*)

The ruins of what was the impressive 13th-century mountain stronghold of Llewelyn the Great can be seen at this site.

Castle Acre Castle (Castle Acre, *Norfolk*)

The remains of a Norman manor house became this castle with earthworks.

Castle Acre Priory (near Castle Acre, *Norfolk*)

The remains of this Cluniac priory include the great west front of the 12th-century church, the prior's lodgings and porch.

Castle Balfour (Lisnaskea, *County Fermanagh*)

This T-plan house with vaulted rooms was built in 1618 and further fortifications were added in 1652. The house has been in ruins since it was damaged by fire in the 1800s.

Castle Bolton (near Richmond, *North Yorkshire*)

This 14th-century castle served as a prison to Mary Queen of Scots for six months.

Castle Campbell (Dollar, *Clackmannanshire*)

The main feature of Castle Campbell, also known as 'Castle Gloom', is the 15th-century tower, which has other buildings built around it. The castle is spectacularly located at the head of Dollar Glen.

Castle Caulfield (Castlecaulfield, *County Tyrone*)

This manor house was built in 1619 by Sir Toby Caulfield, an Oxfordshire knight and ancestor of the Earls of Charlemont. It was built on the site of an ancient fort. The house was damaged by fire in 1641 but was restored and lived in by the Caulfield family until 1670. Saint Oliver Plunkett and John Wesley both preached in the grounds.

Castle Coole (Enniskillen, *County Fermanagh*)

This is one of the finest neo-classical mansions in Ireland. The first mansion was built at great expense for the first Earl of Belmore in the late 18th century. The architect was James Wyatt, Joseph Rose created the plasterwork ceilings and the chimney pieces were by Richard Westmacott.

Castle Fraser (near Dunecht, *Aberdeenshire*)

This splendid baronial tower house was built in 1575 by Michael Fraser, the sixth Laird. The Green Room is rumoured to be haunted by the ghost of a murdered princess.

Castle Grugaig (near Kyle of Lochalsh, *Highland*)

At the remains of this Pictish Iron Age fort near Loch Duich, wall chambers, sections of the staircase and part of the gallery can be seen. The walls of the remains are 2.75 metres (9 feet) thick and 4 metres (13 feet high), and above the doorway there is a large triangular block.

Castle Hedingham (Castle Hedingham, *Essex*)

The village is dominated by the towering Norman keep of Hedingham Castle, which was built in 1140 by the De Vere family who lived here for 500 years.

Castlelaw Hillfort (near Glencorse, *Midlothian*)

This hillfort dates from the Iron Age and has a souterrain (an underground chamber) built in one of the ditches.

Castle Menzies (near Aberfeldy, *Perth and Kinross*)

This late 15th-century castle was the seat of the Menzies clan chief. Today a copy of Bonnie Prince Charlie's death mask can be seen at the castle.

Castle of Old Wick (near Wick, *Highland*)

The remains of an early Norse tower house boast a spectacular site on a rocky outcrop over the sea.

Castlerigg Stone Circle (near Keswick, *Cumbria*)

At this site stand 33 stones to form what is possibly one of the earliest Neolithic stone circles in Britain.

Castle Rising (near King's Lynn, *Norfolk*)

This mid 12th-century keep is set in the centre of huge defensive earthworks. It was once the palace and prison of Isabella, 'She-Wolf', dowager queen of England.

Castle Rushen (Castletown, *Isle of Man*)

Dating from 1153, this medieval fortress stands on the site of a Viking stronghold.

Castle Sween (Loch Sween, *Argyll and Bute*)

Dating from the mid-12th century, Castle Sween is believed to be one of the oldest stone-built castles in Scotland. The tower house and angle tower, which can also be seen, were added to the castle at a later date.

Castle Tioram (near Glenuig, *Highland*)

The shell of this 14th-century castle, which was a Macdonald fortress, can be reached on its rocky islet during low tide. The castle was set on fire by its owner in 1715 to avoid the fortress being captured by the Campbells.

Caterthuns (Brown and White) (near Brechin, *Angus*)

Two impressively large hillforts can be found near the village of Menmuir. Brown Caterthun has four ramparts and ditches as part of its defences and White Caterthun has a sizeable stone rampart, ditches and further outer ramparts.

Cathole Cave *see* PARC LE BREOS.

Cauldside Burn (near Gatehouse of Fleet, *Dumfries and Galloway*)

The remains of two Bronze Age cairns, two stone circles and a carved stone block can be found at the head of Cauldside Burn. The larger of the two stone circles has ten standing stones.

Causey Arch (near Newcastle upon Tyne)

This is the oldest surviving railway bridge in the world. It was built in 1725 to move coal from the mines in horse-drawn trucks.

Cawfields Roman Wall (near Haltwhistle, *Northumberland*)

At this site it is possible to see a well-preserved section of HADRIAN'S WALL, a good section of the vallum earthwork, ditch, camps, turrets, fortlet and Milecastle 42.

Cerne Abbas (Cerne Abbas, *Dorset*)

The gatehouse and tithe barn that belonged to a substantial 10th-century abbey can be seen here. There is also a 55-metre (180-foot) chalk giant on the hill that looks down over the village. The naked figure is 1500 years old and is thought to have been a pagan fertility symbol.

Chapel Royal *see* ST JAMES' PALACE.

Chapterhouse (Westminster Abbey, London)

Built in 1250, the Chapterhouse contains some of the finest medieval English sculpture in existence. The building, which is octagonal in shape, has a central column and still retains the glazed tiles of its original floor.

Charing Cross (West End, London)

The village of Charing lay here in medieval times and the cross was placed here by Edward I in 1290 to mark the final resting place of the funeral cortege of his wife, Eleanor ('chere reine').

Charmouth (Charmouth, *Dorset*)

Charles II took refuge in the Queen's Arms Inn here in 1651 when he was forced into hiding.

Cheddar Gorge (near Axbridge, *Somerset*)

The 10,000 year-old skeleton of the Cheddar Man was discovered in Gough's Cave.

Chedworth Roman Villa (Yanworth, *Gloucestershire*)

This Romano-British villa was built AD 180-350 for a rich landowner. The building is believed to have consisted of three wings enclosing a rectangular courtyard. The bath suites and one of the dining rooms are well-preserved and have fine mosaics. There is evidence of underfloor heating and two forms of bath.

Chepstow Castle (Chepstow, *Monmouthshire*)

This was one of the earliest stone-built castles in Britain and was the centre of the medieval Marches lordship of Chepstow. The castle was extended and altered during the Middle Ages and during the Civil War. Today there are substantial remains that can be seen at this site.

Chester Castle Agricola Tower (Chester, *Cheshire*)

This 12th-century tower, set in the angle of the city walls, contains a fine vaulted chapel.

Chester City Walls (Chester, *Cheshire*)

The town is ringed by medieval walls with Roman and Saxon sections.

Chester Roman Amphitheatre (Chester, *Cheshire*)

This is the largest Roman amphitheatre in Britain. It was used by the 20th Legion, based at the fortress of Deva, for entertainment.

Chesters Bridge (near Low Brunton, *Northumberland*)

On each bank of the North Tyne here it is possible to see remains of the bridge that carried HADRIAN'S WALL across the river. The most impressive remains lie on the east bank, where a stretch of Wall leads from the bridge's east abutment to a gatehouse tower.

Chesters Hillfort (near Drem, *East Lothian*)

An Iron Age hillfort defended by ramparts and ditches, Chesters Hillfort is one of the best-preserved examples of its kind in Scotland.

Chesters Roman Fort (near Chollerton, *Northumberland*)

This fort on HADRIAN'S WALL is one of the best-preserved Roman forts in Britain. The fort is laid out in a rectangle but has round corners. At one time it had two gates on the shorter sides and a main road running between these. It also had two gates on each of the longer sides.

Chetham's Library (Manchester)

Founded in 1653, this was the first free public library in Britain. It occupies the old dormitory of a church residence.

Chichele College (Higham Ferrers, *Northamptonshire*)

This college for secular canons was founded in 1422. Today parts of the quadrangle remain intact.

Chichester (Chichester, *West Sussex*)

The Roman cruciform town plan is still evident in the four-quadrant symmetry of the town centre, and it is surrounded by city walls.

Chingle Hall (near Preston, *Lancashire*)

This cross-shaped and moated house dating from 1260 is Britain's oldest surviving brick-built house.

Chipping Ongar (near Harlow, *Essex*)

The site of an 11th-century castle is marked by a 115-metre (50-foot) mound.

Chirk Castle (Chirk, *Wrexham*)

This is one of a chain of late 13th-century Marches castles. The high walls and drum towers of the castle have remained largely untouched. The inside of the castle reflects the many different styles favoured by its various occupiers.

Chislehurst Caves (Bromley, London)

Over the past 8000 years caves have been hewn out of chalk to create miles of man-made caverns and passages. The remains of a Druid altar and prehistoric fossils can be sen here. The caves were used as a hiding place for Royalists during the Civil War.

Chiswick House (Chiswick, London)

This is one of the original and best English Palladian villas. It was designed by the third Earl of Burlington who was one of the great architects of his time and a great promoter of the Palladian style.

Christchurch (Christchurch, *Dorset*)

The town has the ruins of a castle keep dating from 1100, an ancient priory church founded in 1094 and a tower holding 12 bells, two of which were cast in 1370.

Church of St Hywyn (Aberdaron, *Gwynedd*)

This church dates from the 6th century.

Church of St John the Baptist *see* ST JOHN THE BAPTIST, CHURCH OF.

Church of St Magnus *see* ST MAGNUS, CHURCH OF.

Church of St Mary and St Sexburga *see* ST MARY AND ST SEXBURGA, CHURCH OF.

Church of St Michael *see* ST MICHAEL, CHURCH OF.

Church of the Holy Sepulchre *see* HOLY SEPULCHRE, CHURCH OF.

Chysauster Ancient Village (near Gulval, *Cornwall*)

The well-preserved homes of Iron Age farmers can be seen at this deserted Romano-Cornish village. Eight oval stone houses form what is thought to be England's oldest identifiable village street.

Cilgerran Castle (Cilgerran, *Ceredigion*)

The remains of this castle date from the 11th to 13th centuries. It fell into decay after the Civil War, but the round towers and high walls give an impression of its former strength.

Cille Bharra (Barra, *Western Isles*)

The ruins of the 12th-century Church of St Barr and the restored Chapel of St Mary were once part of Barra's monastery in medieval times.

Cirencester Amphitheatre (Cirencester, *Gloucestershire*)

This and a section of city wall are all that remain of what was the second largest city in Roman Britain, which largely lies buried beneath the modern shopping precinct.

Cissbury Ring (near Bramber, *West Sussex*)

This Iron Age hillfort dating from 300 BC was built on the site previously used by Stone Age man to mine flints.

Clach a'Charridh (near Tain, *Highland*)

This 3-metre (10-foot) carved Pictish stone, called the Stone of Sorrow, is carved with a cross and animals and entwined serpents. Tradition tells that the stone marks the graves of unbaptised infants but no traces have been found to prove this to be true.

Clackmannan Tower (Clackmannan, *Clackmannanshire*)

This 14th-century tower house was once the home of the Bruce family. It boasts a commanding position with views over the Forth Valley.

Clava Cairns (near Inverness, *Highland*)

Dating from the late Neolithic Age, this site has two chambered cairns and a ring cairn forming a row. Each cairn is surrounded by a circle of standing stones.

Claydon House (Middle Claydon, *Buckinghamshire*)

This is the most perfect example of rococo decoration in England. It has a series of rooms with wood carvings in the Chinese and Gothic styles.

Claypotts Castle (near Broughty Ferry, *Angus*)

This 16th-century tower house, built for the Strachan family, is notable for its circular towers that are positioned at opposite corners.

Cleeve Abbey (Washford, *Somerset*)

The well-preserved buildings of a 13th-century Cistercian monastery can be seen at this site. The cloister buildings are intact and include the refectory, which has a splendid timber roof.

Clevedon Court (Clevedon, *North Somerset*)

This 14th-century manor house was once partly fortified and has a 12th-century tower and a 13th-century hall. It is the home of the Eton family.

Clickhimin Broch (near Lerwick, *Shetland*)

A broch tower with secondary buildings dating from the Iron Age.

Clifford's Tower (York, *North Yorkshire*)

This is the 13th-century keep of the ruined York Castle. It is one of the few vestiges of the pair of castles built by William the Conqueror after his victory in 1066.

Clun Castle (Clun, *Shropshire*)
At this site it is possible to see the dramatic ruins of this Norman castle. Remains include the four-storey keep and some other buildings.

Coggleshall Grange Barn (Coggleshall, *Essex*)
This is the oldest surviving timber-framed barn in Europe. It dates from around 1140 and was originally part of the Cistercian monastery of Coggleshall.

Coity Castle (Coity, *Bridgend*)
The remains of this 12th- to 16th-century stronghold include the hall, chapel and part of a square keep.

Colchester (Colchester, *Essex*)
This ancient town is built on the site of a Roman city, founded in AD 50. The huge Norman castle keep was built in 1076 on the site of Roman temple of Claudius.

Conisbrough Castle (Conisbrough, *South Yorkshire*)
This is the oldest circular keep in England and, at 27 metres (90 feet) in height, is one of the finest surviving medieval buildings. It dates from the 12th century.

Conwy Castle (Conwy, *Conwy*)
This castle was built for Edward I between 1283 and 1287. It remains one of the most outstanding achievements of medieval military architecture.

Conwy Town Walls (Conwy, *Conwy*)
These were designed to protect Conwy Castle. They branch out from the castle into a 3-mile (5-kilometre) long circuit that encloses Conwy's ancient quarter. They are punctuated by twenty-one evenly spaced horseshoe towers.

Coombe Castle (Kingston upon Thames, *London*)
This was built by Henry VIII to supply water to HAMPTON COURT PALACE. It consists of two small buildings joined by an underground passage.

Copford Green (Copford Green, *Essex*)

The walls of the remote Norman church here bear framed fragments of human skin, which served as a grim warning in the 9th and 10th centuries when sacrilegious Danes were flayed alive.

Corbridge Roman Site (near Corbridge, *Northumberland*)

This site on HADRIAN'S WALL was originally the site of a fort on a patrol road but later evolved into a principal Roman town and continued to flourish until the 5th century. The impressive ruins include large granaries that have ingenious ventilation systems.

Corfe Castle (Wareham, *Dorset*)

One of the most impressive medieval ruins in England, this former royal castle was where King Edward the Martyr was murdered in 978. It was beseiged by Cromwellians in 1646.

Corgarff Castle (Strathdon, *Aberdeenshire*)

This 16th-century tower house was converted into a barracks for government troops in 1748 in the aftermath of the second Jacobite rising.

Corrimony Chambered Cairn (Drumnadrochit, *Highland*)

This chambered burial cairn is surrounded by a kerb of stone slabs and a circle of eleven standing stones.

Cosmeston Medieval Village (Penarth, *Vale of Glamorgan*)

This village was deserted during the plagues and famines of the 14th century.

Coughton Court (near Alcester, *Warwickshire*)

This impressive central gatehouse dates from 1530. During the Civil War it was attacked by both Parliamentary and Royalist forces. It is believed that the wives of the Gunpowder plotters were here when they heard of the failure of the plan. Under the Tower Room are secret passages that were used as hiding places by priests.

Cowbridge (Cowbridge, *Vale of Glamorgan*)
The remnants of the town's medieval wall and a 13th-century gateway can still be seen.

Cow Tower (Norwich, *Norfolk*)
This 14th-century circular brick tower once formed part of the city defences of Norwich.

Craig Phadrig (near Inverness, *Highland*)
This Iron Age fort is reputed to have been the stronghold of the Pictish King Bude.

Craigievar Castle (near Alford, *Aberdeenshire*)
With its crow-stepped gables, turrets, pink walls and cupolas, Craigievar is often described as a fairy-tale castle. It is an excellent example of Scottish baronial architecture and has remained largely unaltered since it was built in the 17th century.

Craigmillar Castle (City of Edinburgh)
Built in the 1400s, Craigmillar Castle is an L-shaped tower house that was extended in the 16th century. Mary Queen of Scots fled here following the murder of Rizzio.

Craignethan Castle (near Lanark, *South Lanarkshire*)
This is a 16th-century tower house defended by an outer wall and a caponier, an unusual stone-vaulted artillery chamber. It was the inspiration for Tillietudlem Castle in *Old Mortality*, the novel by Sir Walter Scott.

Cranfield Church (Churchtown, *County Antrim*)
There is a famous holy well next to this small, medieval church.

Crathes Castle (near Banchory, *Aberdeenshire*)
This late 16th-century castle was built for the Burnett family. The castle houses collections of family portraits and boasts painted ceilings, the most famous one being in the Room of Nine Nobles, so called because the ceiling is decorated with pictures of great historical figures such as King Arthur and Julius Caesar.

Crediton (Crediton, *Devon*)

This was the Christian centre for Devon in Saxon times and is reputed to be the place where St Boniface was born in AD 680. The cathedral-like church dates from the 15th century.

Criccieth Castle (Criccieth, *Gwynedd*)

The castle is dominated by the twin-towered gatehouse built by Prince Llywelyn ab Iowerth. It was later remodelled by both Edward I and Edward II. It was taken and destroyed by Owain Glyndwr in 1404. Evidence of a fierce fire can still be seen.

Crichton Castle (Pathhead, *Midlothian*)

This is a large castle that was built in the late 14th century and was extended by the Earl of Bothwell in the 16th century when he introduced an unusual Italian-style stonework.

Croft Ambrey (near Leominster, *Hereford and Worcester*)

This Iron Age hillfort dating from 550 BC has ramparts and ditches.

Cromwell's Castle (Tresco, *Isles of Scilly*)

This round tower was built in 1651 to command the haven of New Grimsby.

Crookston Castle (Pollock, Glasgow)

This 15th-century ruined castle consists of a central tower with four square corner towers. The ruin offers wonderful views of the surrounding areas of Glasgow.

Crosby Ravensworth (near Orton, *Cumbria*)

Prehistoric settlements comprising many ruined huts were found at this site.

Crossraguel Abbey (near Maybole, *South Ayrshire*)

The building of this Cluniac abbey began in the 13th century and was founded by the Earl of Carrick. The following three centuries saw the abbey undergo a great deal of rebuilding. Today the remains of the abbey are largely intact, and it is possible to see the church, cloister, chapterhouse, dovecote and living quarters.

Crowland Abbey (Crowland, *Lincolnshire*)

The tower and ruined Norman arch remain of this 12th-century abbey. The bells, dating from the 15th century, are the country's oldest.

Croxden Abbey (near Uttoxeter, *Staffordshire*)

These are the ruins of a Cistercian abbey founded in 1176.

Croy Hill (near Croy, *North Lanarkshire*)

Today there are no visible signs of the fort that stood on this hill, but it is possible to see a pair of beacon platforms and a wall ditch.

Cubbie Row's Castle (Wyre, *Orkney*)

A circular ditch encloses a small rectangular tower at this small keep built by the Norse chief, Klobein Hruga, in 1145. It is reputed to be the oldest stone castle in Scotland.

Cullerlie Stone Circle (near Echt, *Aberdeenshire*)

This Bronze Age site has eight boulders standing in a circle, which has a 9-metre (30-foot) diameter. Inside the circle a number of burial chambers have been excavated.

Culloden Moor (near Inverness, *Highland*)

This is the site of the last battle fought on British soil. On 16 April 1746 the Jacobites, led by Prince Charles Edward Stuart, did battle with the Government troops, led by the Duke of Cumberland, and were defeated. The defeat at Culloden saw the end of the Jacobite uprisings and the beginning of the English 'pacification' of the Highland glens. Today the battlefield is being restored to its original state, and the Graves of the Clans, the Well of the Deac, the Memorial Cairn, the Cumberland Stone and the Field of the English can all be seen.

Culross Palace (Culross, *Fife*)

The palace here was built for Sir George Bruce in the busy

community of Culross during the late 16th and early 17th centuries. Sir George Bruce was instrumental in developing its trading links in coal and salt with other nearby ports.

Culsh Earth House (near Tarland, *Aberdeenshire*)

This Iron Age earth house is approximately 2000 years old and is well preseved, with roofing slabs remaining intact above the large chamber and entrance.

Culzean Castle (near Maybole, *South Ayrshire*)

The castle was built during the 18th century for the tenth Earl of Cassilis and was designed by the great Scottish architect Robert Adam. The castle boasts a cliff-top position and is famed for its splendid oval staircase and circular salon that overlooks the Firth of Clyde.

Cuween Hill Chambered Cairn (near Finstown, *Orkney*)

This Neolithic chambered tomb has four cells and a 5.5-metre (18-foot) passage that on discovery were found to contain the remains of humans, oxen and dogs.

Cymer Abbey (near Llanelltyd, *Gwynedd*)

This Cistercian abbey was founded in 1198 by Maredudd ap Cynan. Remains of the simple abbey church can be seen today.

Cytiau'r Gwyddelod (Holyhead Mountain, *Anglesey*)

The stone foundations of a village found at this site date back 1700 years. Nearby is Caer y Twr, an ancient hillfort.

D

Dalton Castle (Dalton-in-Furness, *Cumbria*)

This is a 14th-century tower that stands in the main street of Dalton-in-Furness.

Danebury Ring (near Andover, *Hampshire*)

At this site are the well-preserved ramparts of an Iron Age fort.

Dane's Dyke (near Bridlington, *North Yorkshire*)

This Stone Age defensive earthwork was in fact completed long before the arrival of the Danes in the 9th century.

Dane's Graves (near Driffield, *North Yorkshire*)

These burial mounds are thought to be the remains of a Celtic tribe dating from the 2nd century. There were once 500 burial mounds at this site but all predate the 9th-century Danish invasion.

Dan-Yr-Ogof Show Caves (Abercraf, *Powys*)

Dan-Yr-Ogof show cave is the longest in Britain. Cathedral Cave is the largest single chamber in a British show cave and Bone Cave was inhabited by human beings 3000 years ago.

Dartmouth Castle (near Dartmouth, *Devon*)

This defensive castle was one of the first castles to be constructed with artillery in mind and has seen 450 years of fortification and preperation for war.

Daventry (Daventry, *Northamptonshire*)

On nearby Borough Hill there is a huge Iron Age fort and Roman excavations. Charles I's army are said to have camped here before the Battle of Naseby in 1645.

Daws Castle (near Watchet, *Somerset*)

This was the site where the inhabitents of the Saxon town of Watchet took refuge against the threat of a Viking attack.

Deal Castle (Deal, *Kent*)

This fort, built by Henry VIII, has huge rounded bastions and once caried 119 guns.

Deddington Castle (Deddington, *Oxfordshire*)

The remains of a 12th-century castle are concealed by extensive earthworks.

Deer Abbey (near Peterhead, *Aberdeenshire*)

The remains of a Cistercian monastery dating from 1219 can be seen at this site.

Denbigh Castle (Denbigh, *Denbighshire*)

This castle was begun in 1282 by Henry de Lacy. It is noted for its impressive gatehouse, which has a trio of towers and a superb archway surmounted by a figure believed to be that of Edward I.

Denbigh Town Walls (Denbigh, *Denbighshire*)

The remains of the town walls, dating from 1282, form an almost complete circuit and include one of the gateways and the unfinished Leicester's Church. Leicester's Church was built by the Earl of Leicester who intended it to become the cathedral of the diocese.

Denby Rigg (near Denby, *North Yorkshire*)

Lying in the hills above Denby are defensive dykes and about 800 cairns dating from 1000 BC.

Denny Abbey (near Cambridge, *Cambridgeshire*)

The remains of the 12th-century Benedictine abbey founded by the Countess of Pembroke can be seen at this site. The abbey was in its time also used by the Knights Templar and Franciscan nuns.

Denton Hall Turret (near Newcastle upon Tyne, *Tyne and Wear*)

At this site there are foundations and a 64-metre (70-yard) section of HADRIAN'S WALL. The turret retains the base of the platform on which the ladders to the upper floors were rested.

Dere Street Roman Road (near Soutra Isle, *Scottish Borders*)

This stretch of Roman Road, which runs from Corbridge by HADRIAN'S WALL to Cramond, near Edinburgh, is quite well preserved. At the roadside it is possible to see pits, evidence of where gravel was taken for building the road.

Derwentcote Steel Furnace (near Newcastle upon Tyne, *Tyne and Wear*)

The earliest and most complete surviving steel works in Britain were built here in the 18th century.

Devenish Island (Devenish Island, *County Fermanagh*)

This island was once the site of a monastery founded in the 6th century by St Molaise, who is regarded as one of the twelve apostles of Ireland. The island is also home to the ruins of Teampull Mor, which dates back to the 13th century, the small 12th-century church, St Molaise's house and 12th-century 24-metre (80-foot) tall round tower. The ruins of St Mary's Augustinian Priory with its carved north chancel door and 15th-century cross can also be seen.

Devil's Ditch (near Burwell, *Suffolk*)

These impressive earthworks cover 7 miles (11 kilometres) and measure 4.5 metres (15 feet) from ditch to bank. It is thought they were built in the post-Roman period to defend Icknield Way, an ancient track from the Wash to Salisbury Plain.

Din Lligwy Ancient Village (Llanallgo, *Anglesey*)

The remains of a 4th-century village can be seen here. The remains include two circular and seven rectangular buildings that still stand up to head height. The buildings are encircled by a pentagonal stone wall, measuring 120 to 150 centimetres (4 to 5) feet thick.

Dirleton Castle (near North Berwick, *East Lothian*)

Part of this attractive castle, built on an outcrop of rock, dates from the 13th century, but much of it was rebuilt and extended in the 14th and 16th centuries. The castle gardens boast a 17th-century bowling green.

Dogton Stone (near Kirkcaldy, *Fife*)

Lying approximately $1^1/_2$ miles (2.5 kilometres) northeast of Cardenden railway station, the Dogton Stone is an example of a free-standing cross-slab.

Dolaucothi Gold Mines (Pumsaint, *Carmarthenshire*)

This is the only place in Britain where the Romans mined for gold.

Dolbadarn Castle (Llanberis, *Gwynedd*)

This castle was built in the early 13th century by the Welsh leader Llewelyn the Great.

Dolwyddelan Castle (near Dolwyddelan, *Conwy*)

The square stone keep dates from the 13th century and is all that remains of the castle built by Llywelyn ab Iorwerth. Edward I remodelled the site during his reign.

Donnington Castle (near Newbury, *Berkshire*)

Surviving amongst some impressive earthworks is the twin-towered gatehouse of the castle. It is thought to date from the late 14th century.

Doonhill Homestead (near Dunbar, *East Lothian*)

This site is unsual as it is a record of the Anglian occupation of southeast Scotland. On this site the remains of 6th-century wooden hall of a British chief and of the superceding Anglian chief's 7th-century hall were excavated in the 1960s.

Dorset Cursus (near Cashmoor, *Dorset*)

These Neolithic earthworks, thought to have been a religious ceremonial route, stretch for several miles and consist of two parallel banks flanked with barrows.

Doune Castle (Doune, *Stirling*)

This well-preserved 14th-century courtyard castle was built for the Regent Albany. The castle, four storeys high, is surrounded by a moat and is noted for its gatehouse tower, which is 29 metres (95 feet) high.

Dover Castle (Dover, *Kent*)

Below the ancient fortress of Dover Castle run miles of tunnels that were first used during the Napoleonic wars and were later used as an information nerve centre during World War II.

Down House (Downe, *Kent*)

This was the home of Charles Darwin for more than forty years and where he worked on his ground-breaking theories.

Dozmary Pool (Colliford Lake, near Bodmin, *Cornwall*)

According to local legend this is the pool into which Sir Bedevere hurled King Arthur's sword, Excalibur, after Arthur's death. It is claimed that the sword was then raised from the depths by an emerging hand.

Druchtag Motte (Mochrum, *Dumfries and Galloway*)

In the 12th and 13th centuries, motte castles were prolific in this area of Scotland. This timber castle is a good example of one of them.

Druid's Altar *see* **Ballyumford**.

Drumena Cashel (Castlewellan, *County Down*)

This is one of the best-preserved stone ring forts in Ireland. The fort dates back to early Christian times and has an underground stone-built passage that is thought to have been used as a place of safety and for storage.

Drumtroddan Cup and Ring Marks (near Port William, *Dumfries and Galloway*)

The cup and ring marks carved into the bedrock here are thought to date from the Bronze Age.

Drumtroddan Standing Stones (near Port William, *Dumfries and Galloway*)

Near to the Drumtroddan cup and ring marks is a group of three standing stones, one of which has fallen over.

Dryburgh Abbey (near Melrose, *Scottish Borders*)

The ruins of this 12th-century abbey are well preserved. The abbey was sacked by English invaders in the 14th and 16th centuries. Sir Walter Scott and Field Marshal Sir Douglas Haig are buried in the abbey.

Dryslwyn Castle (Dryslwyn, *Carmarthenshire*)

This ruined 13th-century castle was a stronghold of the native Welsh. It played an important role during the struggles between the Welsh and the English.

Duart Castle (near Craignure, Mull, *Argyll and Bute*)

This MacLean stronghold was built in the 13th century on a cliff top. Over a period of three centuries various additions were made and the castle boasts a hundred rooms.

Duff House (near Banff, *Aberdeenshire*)

This early Georgian mansion was designed for the Earl of Fife by William Adam and is thought to be his finest work and one of the best examples of Georgian baroque architecture in Britain..

Duffus Castle (near Elgin, *Moray*)

This motte-and-bailey castle was the seat of the Moray family and is the finest example of this type of castle in the north of Scotland.

Duggleby Howe (near North Grimston, *North Yorkshire*)

Eight adults and two children were buried with their belongings in this Stone Age mound. Four-thousand-year-old tools made from deer antlers were also found at this site.

Dumbarton Castle (Dumbarton, *West Dunbartonshire*)

This is the site of the ancient capital of Strathclyde. The castle ruins are spectacularly set on the volcanic Dumbarton Rock above the River Clyde. The remains include the Wallace Tower, thought to date from the 5th century. At the foot of the Rock are 18th-century artillery fortifications and barracks and a sundial given to the town by Mary Queen of Scots.

Dunadd Fort (Poltalloch Estate, *Argyll and Bute*)

This historic site has been occupied since the Iron Age. The stone walls of a well-preserved ancient fort are thought to be post-Roman. There are also carvings on the rock face that mark a Pictish victory in ad 683.

Dunaverty Rock (near Campbeltown, *Argyll and Bute*)

This is the site of old Dunaverty Castle, which was formerly a Macdonald stronghold. In 1647 a garrison of 300 was beseiged here by Covenanters. On surrender each of the defenders was slain, and so this site is known as Blood Rock.

Dunblane Cathedral (Dunblane, *Stirling*)

This splendid cathedral dates from the 13th century and it is one of Scotland's noblest medieval churches, although only the choir survived the Reformation. It was restored in the early 20th century and features fine wood carving in the pews.

Dun Carloway Broch (near Carloway, Lewis, *Western Isles*)

This Iron Age stone fort is thought to have been built 1700 years ago. The fort has a large courtyard surrounded by double walls, between which are stairs, chambers and galleries. Some of the 9-metre (30-foot) walls are still standing.

Dunchraigaig Cairn (near Kilmartin, *Argyll and Bute*)

This Bronze Age cairn has had its covering stones removed to reveal three burial cists.

Dundonald Castle (Dundonald, *South Ayrshire*)

This large stone castle was built in the 1370s by Robert II ('King Bob'). The castle has two feasting halls, one directly above the other, with vaults beneath. This site also has the remains of a 13th-century Stewart castle, and there is evidence that the hill was the site of a large fort during the Dark Ages.

Dundrennan Abbey (near Kirkcudbright, *Dumfries and Galloway*)

The ruins of this Cistercian abbey, founded in 1142 by David I, are still attractive to this day. The east end of the church and the chapterhouse are noted for their architectural quality. Dundrennan Abbey is where Mary Queen of Scots spent her last night in Scotland in May 1568.

Dundrum Castle (Newcastle, *County Down*)

This is one of the finest medieval castles in Ireland. It was built in 1177 by John de Courcy on a site overlooking Dundrum Bay. The castle was captured in 1210 by King John and was badly damaged in 1652 by Cromwell's troops. The ruined remains include a huge round keep, with 16-metre (52-foot) high walls, which is surrounded by a curtain wall. The remains of a 13th-century gatehouse can also be seen.

Duneight Motte and Bailey (Lisburn, *County Antrim*)

This impressive Anglo-Norman earthwork castle has a high mound-embanked enclosure that is based on the defences of an earlier fort.

Dunfallandy Stone (near Pitlochry, *Perth and Kinross*)

This fine Pictish sculptured stone has a cross on one face and figures on both faces.

Dunfermline Abbey and Palace (Dunfermline, *Fife*)

The remains of the 11th-century Benedictine abbey, founded by Queen Margaret, are substantial. Robert the Bruce, famous 14th-century king of Scotland, is buried in the choir. Next to the abbey are the ruins of the royal palace built for James VI and I, which was the birthplace of Charles I, the last monarch to be born in Scotland.

Dun Fiadhairt (Loch Dunvegan, Skye, *Highland*)

This Iron Age broch is thought to be 2000 years old. The walls contain guardrooms at each side of the entrance and are 3.6 metres (12 feet) thick.

Dungiven Priory (Dungiven, *County Londonderry*)

Dungiven was the stronghold of the O'Cahan chiefs until the 17th century. It was the O'Cahans who founded this Augustinian priory in 1150. The church was greatly altered in later centuries. It contains one of the finest medieval tombs in Northern Ireland. The tomb is that of Cooey na Gail O'Cahan who died in 1385. A sculpted effigy of Cooney na Gail, dressed in Irish armour, lies under a stonework canopy and below this are six kilted warriors.

Dun Grugaig (near Loch Hourn, *Highland*)

On the cliff top the remains of an Iron Age fort can be found.

The defensive wall is 2.4 metres (8 feet) high and 4.25 metres (14 feet) thick, and has internal chambers and an entrance passage.

Dunham Massey White Cottage (Little Bollington, *Cheshire*)

This important timber-framed cottage was built as a cruck-trussed open hall in about 1500 and was later altered in the 17th century

Dunkeld Cathedral (Dunkeld, *Perth and Kinross*)

This ruined cathedral dates from the 12th century. The 14th-century choir is now home to the parish church.

Dunluce Castle (Portballintrae, *County Antrim*)

This 16th-century castle was once the stronghold of the MacQuillans and MacDonnells who adapted an earlier stone-built fortress. A house was built in the centre of the castle by Randal MacDonnell. Parts of the Great Hall, towers and 17th-century gatehouse remain. The castle is in ruins today. A cave that lies beneath the castle ruins provided a secret passage to and from the castle from the sea.

Dunottar Castle (near Stonehaven, *Aberdeenshire*)

This dramatic castle ruin stands proudly on a solitary rock on the beach. The castle was a Royalist stronghold and was captured by Cromwell's troops after months of siege in 1652.

Dunscaith Castle (near Tokavaig, Skye, *Highland*)

This is one of the oldest fortified headlands in this area of Scotland. The remains of this former home of the MacDonald clan are well preserved.

Dunsinane (near Perth, *Perth and Kinross*)

This Iron Age hillfort, which is enclosed by a rampart, is thought to have been the site of Macbeth's castle.

Dunstaffnage Castle (near Oban, *Argyll and Bute*)

The remains of this 13th-century castle are set on rock on the shore of Loch Etive and include a great curtain wall. In medieval times the castle was governed by the Campbells. Nearby are the remains of a chapel.

Dunstanburgh Castle (near Alnwick, *Northumberland*)

The skeletal ruins of this huge 14th-century castle stand on the cliffs above the North Sea. The ruins include the gatehouse and curtain walls. The building of the castle was initiated by John the Gaunt, but it had fallen into ruins by Tudor times.

Duntulm Castle (near Kilmuir, Skye, *Highland*)

This 17th-century castle was built on a cliff by the MacDonalds on the site of a Celtic hillfort.

Dunvegan Castle (Loch Dunvegan, Skye, *Highland*)

This castle on Loch Dunvegan has been the main MacLeod stronghold since the early 13th century. Its Fairy Tower, dating from the beginning of the 16th century, accommodated both Dr Johnson and Sir Walter Scott in visits to the castle.

Dunyvaig Castle (South Islay, *Highland*)

This ruined fortress in the Inner Hebrides dates back to the 14th century and once belonged to the MacDonalds, Lords of the Isles.

Dupath Well (near Callington, *Cornwall*)

This almost complete granite-built well house is set over a holy well dating from *c.*1500.

Durham Cathedral (Durham, *County Durham*)

The cathedral stands on the site of an early Saxon cathedral, which was built to house the remains of St Cuthbert. The present cathedral was completed in 1133 and has survived mostly intact. It is an excellent example of the Norman-Romanesque style. The remains of St Cuthbert lie beneath a marble slab in the Shrine of St Cuthbert. His remains were exhumed for reburial in 1104 and his body was found to be completely uncorrupted more than 400 years after his death on LINDISFARNE.

Duxford Chapel (Whittlesford, *Cambridgeshire*)

This medieval chapel was once part of the Hospital of St John.

Dwarfie Stane (Hoy, *Orkney*)

A Neolothic burial chamber has been cut into a huge sandstone block at this site. Legend tells that the tomb is home to the malevolant dwarf of Norse sagas.

Dyce Symbol Stones (near Dyce, *Aberdeenshire*)

In the ruined parish church of St Fergus are two Pictish stones. One has incised symbols while the other has symbols and a Celtic cross.

Dymchurch Martello Tower (Dymchurch, *Kent*)

This is one of the many artillery towers that were built to resist the anticipated invasion of Napoleon.

Dynevor Castle (Llandeilo, *Carmarthenshire*)

The massive 13th-century keep of this castle stands among the ruins on the cliffs above the Tywi river.

Dyrham Park (Dyrham Park, *South Gloucestershire*)

This house was built between 1691 and 1710 for William Blathwayt, Secretary of State to William III. The rooms have remained largely unchanged since they were first furnished.

E

Earl's Palace (Birsay, *Orkney*)

The remains of the residence of the late 16th-century Earl of Orkney can be seen at this site.

Earn's Heugh (near St Abb's Head, *Scottish Borders*)

On the cliff near St Abb's Head, Iron Age hillforts can be found with banks, ditches and the foundations of circular huts.

Easby Abbey (near Richmond, *North Yorkshire*)

The remains of this medieval abbey stand by the River Swale.

Eassie Sculptured Stones (near Glamis, *Angus*)

This monument is elaborately sculptured with cross and figures carved on one side and processional scenes on the other.

East Gate (Bath, *Bath and North East Somerset*)

This is the only surviving medieval gateway into the city of Bath.

East Gate (Gloucester, *Gloucestershire*)

An underground chamber displays the remains of Roman gate towers and the medieval wall and moat.

East Wemyss (East Wemyss, *Fife*)

Northeast of the village on the cliff top sits a red-sandstone castle thought to have been the stronghold of the Macduff thanes of Fife. In the caves beneath the castle the walls bear inscriptions that show that it was occupied from the Bronze Age.

Edgehill (near Kineton, *Warwickshire*)

Charles I's army gathered here for battle and the king raised his standard here in 1642.

Edin's Hall Broch (near Grantshouse, *Scottish Borders*)

On the northeastern slope of Cockburn's Law lie the remains of an unsually large Iron Age broch, one of the few remaining in Lowland Scotland. The broch is defended by ramparts and ditches and is partially overlain by later settlements.

Edinburgh Castle (City of Edinburgh)

This is one of the most famous castles in Scotland. It has been the home of Scottish kings and queens over past centuries. Mary Queen of Scots gave birth to James VI and I in the Old Royal Palace where the Scottish Crown Jewels are now kept. The castle also houses the famous 15th-century gun, Mons Meg, and the oldest building in Edinburgh, the 12th-century St Margaret's Chapel.

Edlingham Castle (Edlingham, *Northumberland*)

This complex ruin is noted for its defensive features spanning the 13th-15th centuries.

Edvin Loach Old Church (near Bromyard, *Hereford and Worcester*)

The remains of an 11th-century church can be seen at this site.

Edzell Castle (Edzell, *Angus*)

The red-sandstone ruins of this 16th-century L-plan castle are dominated by a late medieval tower house and walls of the Great Hall. The garden walls have carved early 17th-century Renaissance decorations that are unique in Britain.

Egglestone Abbey (near Barnard Castle, *County Durham*)

Substantial parts of the church and abbey buildings remain from this 12th-century abbey.

Eleanor Cross (Geddington, *Northamptonshire*)

This is one of a series of the crosses erected by Edward I to mark the resting places of the body of his wife, Eleanor, when it was brought from Harby to Westminster Abbey for burial.

Elgin Cathedral (Elgin, *Moray*)

The ruins of what is considered to be Scotland's most splendid cathedral are still superb today. The church was burned by the Wolf of Badenoch in 1390. The Celtic cross-slab in the choir has Pictish symbols carved on it.

Eliseg's Pillar (near Llangollen, *Denbighshire*)

This is an ancient memorial stone to Eliseg, the 9th-century chief of the house of Powys. The pillar stands on the burial mound of a 5th- or 6th-century chieftan.

Elizabethan House (Plymouth, *Devon*)

This is a rare, surviving Tudor sea captain's timber-framed house lying in the heart of Plymouth's historic Barbican.

Eltham Palace (Eltham, Greater London)

This was the favourite country retreat of English kings from the time of Henry III to Henry VIII. Although largely rebuilt in the 20th century, it still retains a stone bridge over the moat and the banqueting hall's splendid 15th-century oak roof.

Ely Cathedral (Ely, *Cambridgeshire*)

St Etheldreda founded an abbey here in AD 670. A Norman cathedral was built on the site in 1083, and Norman remains can still be seen in the west front, nave and transepts. An octagonal lantern tower was added in 1322.

Escomb (near Bishop Auckland, *County Durham*)

The well-preserved Saxon church here was built using Roman stones and contains a 13th-century carving of a knight.

Etal Castle (Etal, *Northumberland*)

At this site it is possible to see the ruined gatehouse of a 14th-century border castle.

Eton College (Eton, *Berkshire*)

This school was founded in 1440 by Henry IV.

Eton College Chapel (Eton, *Berkshire*)

This is one of the finest examples of Perpendicular architecture. Dating from 1483, it was planned by Henry IV and was intended to be the choir of a church to rival Canterbury, but only the choir was completed.

Ewenny Priory (near Bridgend, *Bridgend*)

This ruined priory was founded in 1141 by Maurice de Londres. The massive walls date from the 13th century. In the church vault there are tomb slabs bearing Norman inscriptions.

Ewloe Castle (Ewloe, *Flintshire*)

This was a native Welsh castle, and Henry II was defeated nearby in 1157. The remains include part of the Welsh Tower, a well, remnants of wall and another tower.

Eynsford Castle (Eynsford, *Kent*)

This was one of the first castles to be built in Britain by the Normans. Today it is possible to see the moat and the remains of of the curtain wall and hall.

F

Falkland Palace (Falkland, *Fife*)

This palace was built between 1501 and 1541 by James IV and James V, and it replaced earlier castle and palace buildings dating from the 12th century. It was the favourite seat of Mary Queen of Scots and James V. The grounds house the oldest real tennis court in Britain.

Farleigh Hungerford Castle (Farleigh Hungerford, *Somerset*)

The ruins of this 14th-century castle house a chapel containing wall paintings, stained glass and the tomb of the castle's builder, Sir Thomas Hungerford.

Farne Islands (*Northumberland*)

St Cuthbert died on Inner Farne in 687, and there is a chapel built in his memory dating from the 14th century.

Farnham Castle Keep (near Farnham, *Surrey*)

This motte-and-bailey castle was once one of the seats of the Bishop of Winchester. It has been been occupied since the 12th century.

Faversham Stone Chapel (near Faversham, *Kent*)

The remains of this small medieval church incorporate a Romano-British pagan mausoleum dating from the 4th century.

Fayfield Down (near Marlborough, *Wiltshire*)

This was the source of many of the stones used to build STONEHENGE. This area has been farmed since 700 BC, and the outlines of Celtic fields can still be seen.

Felin Isaf Watermill (Glan-Conwy, *Conwy*)

This 17th-century mill has a working water wheel and has recently been restored.

Fiddleford Manor (near Sturminster, *Dorset*)

Part of this medieval manor house remains intact. The fine roof structures and upper living room are the best in this part of the country.

Finchale Priory (near Durham, *County Durham*)

This 13th-century Wearside ruin was built on the site of a hermitage founded by St Godric, a reformed pirate. A cross on the floor marks his tomb.

Findlater Castle (near Cullen, *Aberdeenshire*)

This cliff-side castle, now in ruins, was built by the Ogilvie family in medieval times and was inhabited until the early 17th century.

Finlaggan Castle (Islay, *Argyll and Bute*)

Although now ruined, this castle in the Inner Hebrides was once the administrative centre, parliament and ancient seat of the Lords of the Isles. It was from here that Clan Donald chiefs dominated expanses of the Atlantic in the 14th–15th centuries.

Finovan Doocot (near Forfar, *Angus*)

This is the largest dovecote in Scotland and has 2400 nesting boxes. It is believed to have been built by an Earl of Crawford in the 16th century.

Fishbourne Roman Palace (Fishbourne, *West Sussex*)

These remains of the largest Roman residence to be found north of the Alps feature some of the finest mosaics discovered in northern Europe.

Fishguard (Fishguard, *Pembrokeshire*)

A stone recalls the last invasion of British soil. In 1797 French invaders surrendered here after they mistook local women in red dresses for red-coated soldiers.

Flat Howe *see* HIGH BRIDESTONES.

Flint Castle (Flint, *Flintshire*)

This castle was started by Edward I in 1277. It is noted for its great tower or donjon, which is separated from the castle by a moat. It is thought that this tower would have been the chief residence of the castle. The remains also include part of the walls and corner towers of the inner bailey.

Flodden Field (near Coldstream, *Scottish Borders*)

A tall cross in a field marks the site of the 1513 Battle of Flodden when the English routed the Scots. About 10,000 people were killed in the battle, many of whom are buried in St Paul's Church at Branxton, nearby.

Florence Court (Enniskillen, *County Fermanagh*)

This 18th-century mansion is named after the wife of John Cole, the father of the first Earl of Enniskillen. The mansion is noted for its interior rococo plasterwork. The fine gardens contain the Florence Court Yew—mother of all Irish yews.

Flowerdown Barrows (Littleton, *Hampshire*)

At this site it is possible to see the round barrows of a Bronze Age burial site.

Forde Abbey (near Chard, *Somerset*)

This 12th-century Cistercian abbey is adorned with fine Tudor stonework and a notable collection of tapestries.

Fort Charlotte (Lerwick, *Shetland*)

This five-sided artillery fort was built in 1665 to protect the Sound of Bressay from the Dutch, but it was burned by the Dutch in 1673. It was rebuilt in 1781.

Fort Cumberland (Portsmouth, *Hampshire*)

This fort was built in the shape of a wide pentagon by the Duke of Cumberland in 1746. It is considered to be the most impressive piece of 18th-century defensive architecture remaining in England.

Fort George (near Nairn, *Highland*)

This vast site is home to one of the most impressive artillery fortifications in Europe. It was planned in 1747 as a base for

George II's army after the second Jacobite Rebellion and was completed in 1769.

Fortrose Cathedral (Fortrose, *Highland*)

The remains of the cathedral that was built here between the 13th and 15th centuries and probably destroyed by Cromwell retain some vaulting.

Fotheringhay (Fotheringhay, *Cambridgeshire*)

A grassy mound marks the site of the castle in which Mary Queen of Scots was executed in 1587.

Fountains Abbey and Studley Royal Water Garden (near Ripon, *North Yorkshire*)

This is one of the most remarkable sites in Europe. Fountains Abbey and Studley Royal encompass the spectacular ruin of a 12th-century Cistercian abbey, a Jacobean mansion and one of the best-preserved examples of a Georgian green water garden.

Fowlis Wester Sculptured Stone (Fowlis Wester, *Perth and Kinross*)

The stone stands in the village church and a replica stands in the square. The stone is a tall cross-slab carved with Pictish symbols.

Framlingham Castle (Framlingham, *Suffolk*)

This splendid 12th-century castle retains much of its original exterior. The continuous curtain wall links thirteen towers. In its time the castle has had various uses, including those of an Elizabethan prison, a poor house and a school.

Freshwater East (Freshwater East, *Pembrokeshire*)

The dunes at this beach cover Stone Age and Bronze Age sites.

Frithelstock (Frithelstock, *Devon*)

North Devon's only monastic ruin lies next to the church in which there are medieval pews carved with the figures of two priests sticking out their tongues.

Furness Abbey (near Barrow-in-Furness, *Cumbria*)

This is one of Cumbria's finest ruins, with its set of roofless red-sandstone arcades and pillars. At one time it was the most powerful abbey in the northwest, owning a large part of southern Cumbria, the Isle of Man and some land in Ireland. In fact, it was so wealthy that it was twice raided by the Scottish. It survived until Henry VIII decided that it should be one of the first abbeys to be dissolved.

Fyvie Castle (Fyvie, *Aberdeenshire*)

Each of the five towers of Fyvie Castle is named after one of the five families who owned the castle (Preston, Meldrum, Seton, Gordon and Leith). The oldest part of the castle dates from the 15th century. The castle is an excellent example of Scottish baronial architecture.

G

Gainsborough Old Hall (Gainsborough, *Lincolnshire*)

This large medieval house has a splendid Great Hall and a suite of rooms. It houses a collection of historic furniture.

Gainsthorpe Medieval Village (near Hibaldstow, *North Lincolnshire*)

This hidden village has outlines in turf of earthworks, peasant houses, gardens and streets.

Gallox Bridge (Dunster, *Somerset*)

This stone packhorse bridge, which spans the old mill stream, has two ribbed arches.

Garrison Church (Portsmouth, *Hampshire*)

This was founded in 1212 as a hospice for travellers, the elderly and the sick. Charles II and Catherine of Braganza were married here in 1662.

Garrison Walls (St Mary's, *Isles of Scilly*)

At this site it is possible to see the remains of the walls and earthworks that were built as part of the island's defences.

Garynahine (Lewis, *Western Isles*)

On this site in the Outer Hebrides there is a stone slab surrounded by a ring of boulders that in turn are surrounded by a ring of upright stone slabs, the tallest of which is 2.75 metres (9 feet) tall.

General Kay's monument *see* **Caiy Stone**.

George Inn (Southwark, London)

This is the only galleried inn remaining in London. It was famous as a coaching inn in the 17th century.

Giant's Cave (Broad Down, Worcester, *Hereford and Worcester*)

A Welsh prince fleeing the English is said to have sheltered here in 1405.

Giant's Ring (Belfast)

This circular Bronze Age enclosure measures nearly 61 metres (200 feet) in diameter. It is similar in style to STONEHENGE and has a stone chambered grave in the centre that is surrounded by 4-metre (12-foot) high banks. This site is thought to have been used for ritual burials but little else is known about it. In the 18th century it was used as a horse racing circuit.

Gib Hill Barrow *see* ARBOR LOW STONE CIRCLE.

Gilsland (Gilsland, *Northumberland*)

This well-preserved milecastle on HADRIAN'S WALL has 3-metre (10-foot) high walls.

Glamis Castle (Glamis, *Angus*)

The six-storey tower dates from the 15th century but much of the rest of the castle is of the 17th century. This was the childhood home of the Queen Elizabeth the Queen Mother and the birthplace of Princess Margaret, and it is thought to be the most haunted stately home in Britain.

Glasgow Cathedral (City of Glasgow)

This is the only medieval cathedral on the Scottish mainland that survived the Reformation intact. It is built over the tomb of St Kentigern, and one of its outstanding features is the elaborately vaulted crypt.

Glastonbury (Glastonbury, *Somerset*)

This is the legendary site of King Arthur's island paradise, Avalon. It is said that he and his queen, Guinevere, are buried among the ruins of the 13th-century abbey ruins. It is also believed by some that the Holy Grail lies below Chalice Spring on Glastonbury Tor.

Glastonbury Tribunal (Glastonbury, *Somerset*)

This well-preserved medieval town house is thought to have been used as the courthouse of GLASTONBURY ABBEY.

Glebe Cairn (Kilmartin, *Argyll and Bute*)

At this site it is possible to see a Bronze Age cairn with two burial chambers.

Glenbuchat Castle (near Alford, *Aberdeenshire*)

Built in 1590, this is a fine example of a Z-plan tower house. The last laird, John Gordon, was a notable Jacobite.

Glencoe (Glencoe, *Highland*)

A stone cross marks the site of the Massacre of Glencoe. On 13 February 1692, 38 members of the Clan MacDonald were murdered by their guests, the Campbells. The MacDonalds were Jacobites and the Campbells were supporters of the English king, but the Campbells were shown hospitality by the MacDonalds as it was Highland custom that no one would be refused food and shelter. The Campbells' abuse of this custom and the 'murder under trust' shocked all Scotland.

Glenelg Brochs (near Kyle of Lochalsh, *Highland*)

At this site two broch towers stand over 9 metres (30 feet) tall. Each tower has well-preserved structural features.

Glenfinnan Monument (Glenfinnan, *Highland*)

This monument was erected in 1815 on the spot where the Highland army gathered to see Bonnie Prince Charlie raise the standard of rebellion in August 1745. It was erected by Alexander MacDonald in memory of the clansmen who died during the rebellion.

Glenluce Abbey (near Glenluce, *Dumfries and Galloway*)

This is a Cistercian abbey that was founded in 1192. Today it is possible to see the remains of a handsome early 16th-century chapterhouse.

Gloucester Cathedral (Gloucester, *Gloucestershire*)

This was built in 1089 to replace an earlier abbey. The transepts and choir, remodelled in the 14th century, are amongst the earliest examples of Perpendicular architecture. The 14th-century east window is the largest stained-glass window in Britain and was created as a memorial to those who died at the Battle of Crecy in 1346. In the north arcade of the presbytery stands the elaborately carved tomb of Edward II, dating from the 14th century. It stands next to the tomb of King Osric who founded the first abbey in AD 681. There is also the 12th-century tomb of Robert, Duke of Normandy, son of William the Conqueror.

Goodmanham (near Beverley, *East Riding of Yorkshire*)

A Norman church stands here on the site of a 7th-century pagan temple. The high priest of the temple, Coifi, was converted to Christianity in AD 627.

Goodrich Castle (near Ross-on-Wye, *Hereford and Worcester*)

This surprisingly intact red-sandstone castle has a 12th-century keep and remains from the 13th and 14th centuries.

Grain Earth House (near Kirkwall, *Orkney*)

This site boasts a well-built Iron Age earth house that has an underground chamber supported on stone pillars.

Grantham (Grantham, *Lincolnshire*)

Richard III signed the Duke of Buckingham's death warrant here in 1483 at the ancient Angel and Royal, which was one of the historic staging posts on the Great North Road.

Great Coxwell Barn (Great Coxwell, *Oxfordshire*)

This 13th-century stone-built monastic barn has a stone-tiled roof and an interesting timber structure.

Great Mount (Stebbing, *Essex*)

This earthwork is the site of a castle built in 1086 by Ranulf Peveral.

Great Witcombe Roman Villa (near Gloucester, *Gloucestershire*)

At the remains of this large Roman villa it is possible to see fine renovated mosaic pavements and the luxurious bath house complex.

Greencastle (Kilkeel, *County Down*)

This 13th-century royal fortress has a massive keep, a gatehouse and a curtain wall. It is similar in appearance to an English Norman castle. The castle was besieged and taken by Edward Bruce in 1316 and then taken twice in the 14th century by the Irish. It was then maintained as a garrison for Elizabeth I in the 1590s.

Greenknowe Tower (near Gordon, *Scottish Borders*)

This handsome L-shaped tower house was built in 1581 by James Seton. The tower's clockwise staircase was one of its main defensive features as it gave defenders the advantage of an unhindered sword arm while attackers would be at a disadvantage.

Gretna Green (Gretna Green, *Dumfries and Galloway*)

This village was made famous when runaway couples from England came here to be married under Scots law, which allowed them to be married by a simple decleration before witnesses. This form of marriage was made illegal in 1940.

Grey Abbey (Ballywalter, *County Down*)

This Cistercian abbey was founded in 1193 by Affreca, daughter of a king of the Isle of Man. The ruins of the abbey are among the best preserved in Northern Ireland and include the chancel with its lancet windows, splendid west doorway and effigy tomb—thought be that of Affreca. In 1572 the abbey was burned down and was later used as a parish church.

Grey Cairns of Camster (near Camster, *Highland*)

These two well-preseved burial chambers date from the New Stone Age, which began 6000 years ago. One of the cairns is long, measuring nearly 60 metres (200 feet), and has two chambers and projecting 'horns'. The other cairn is round and has a single chamber. When the cairns were discovered they were found to contain legless skeletons.

Greyfriars (Gloucester, *Gloucestershire*)

At this site it is possible to see the remains of a late 15th /early 16th-century Franciscan friary church.

Greyfriars Kirk (City of Edinburgh)

In 1638 a large crowd gathered in the churchyard of Greyfriars Kirk to sign the National Covenant, rejecting Anglicanism, professing loyalty to the king but asserting Scotland's right to determine its own religion. From this were born the Covenanters, who played a significant role in the bloody 17th-century religious wars.

Greyfriars Kirk is also the burial place of John Gray, the owner of Edinburgh's most famous dog, Greyfriar's Bobby, who watched over his owner's grave for fourteen years and was cared for by local residents.

Grime's Graves (near Thetford, *Norfolk*)

Unique in England, these outstanding Neolithic flint mines consist of over thirty pits and shafts. The flint extracted from these mines was used to make axes and knives.

Grimspound (Dartmoor, *Devon*)

The remains of twenty-four huts can be seen at this late Bronze Age settlement. The settlement covers an area of four acres and is enclosed by a stone wall.

Grosmont Castle (Grosmont, *Monmouthshire*)

This is one of the 'trilateral' castles of Hubert de Burgh, built to guard the approaches to the Welsh mountains, the others being SKENFRITH and WHITE CASTLE. The remains here include the dry moat, the 13th-century great hall and the western curtain wall.

Guildhall of Corpus Christi (Lavenham, Sudbury, *Suffolk*)

This late 15th-century timber-framed Tudor building was originally the hall of the Guild of Corpus Christi.

Guisborough Priory (Guisborough, *Redcar and Cleveland*)

The remains of this Augustinian priory include the gatehouse and the east end of an early 14th-century church.

Gurness Broch (Mainland, *Orkney*)

Standing on a headland overlooking the island of Rousay, this 2000-year-old dry-stone tower has an underground chamber that is still visible today as well as an upper gallery and floor.

Gwydir Castle (Llanrwst, *Conwy*)

An early 16th-century house that was for many years the main residence of the Wynn family. It was added to over the centuries but was badly damaged by fire in the 20th century and subsequently restored.

Gwydir Uchaf Chapel (Llanrwst, *Conwy*)

This chapel was built in the 17th century by Sir John Wynn of Gwydir Castle and is noted for its painted ceiling and varied woodwork.

H

Hackness Mortello Tower (Hoy, *Orkney*)

This is one of a pair of towers that were built in the early 19th century to provide protection to British convoys from French and American privateers. The tower was a base for a 24-pounder cannon and its crew.

Hadleigh Castle (near Hadleigh, *Essex*)

Of this 13th-century castle the curtain wall and two towers survive.

Hadrian's Wall (*Northumberland/Cumbria*)

Hadrian's Wall divided the 'civilized' world of the Romans from the northern tribes. Emperor Hadrian, who toured Roman Britain in AD 122, wanted the Roman empire to live at peace within stable frontiers, the majority of which were defined by geographical features. The north of Roman Britain had no such natural barrier and so he decided to create a man-made barrier, a wall 73 miles (117 kilometres) long, stretching from the Tyne to the Solway Firth. It was built as a base for patrols that could push into the hostile territory and to serve as a deterrent to the the northern tribes. The Wall linked the existing system of forts and watchtowers along the Stanegate road. The Wall was punctuated by milecastles (small forts) with turrets positioned between them. To the front of the Wall there was a deep ditch running in parallel and behind this a great earthwork or *vallum* stretching along its entire length. Major modifications were made before the Wall was finished, and the bulk of the garrison were moved into the Wall to occupy forts at 6 to 9 mile (10 to 14.5 kilometre) intervals. The Wall's garrison were positioned in a few key areas and were closer to the enemy and so were able to quickly respond to any attack. This structure remained in operation until the Romans left in AD 411.

Hailes Abbey (near Winchcombe, *Gloucestershire*)

This Cistercian abbey was founded in 1246 by Richard, Earl of Cornwall. It became a gentleman's residence after the dissolution of the monasteries and fell into ruins in 1800.

Hailes Castle (near East Linton, *East Lothian*)

This delightfully sited ruin incorporates a 13th-century fortified manor that was extended in the 14th and 15th centuries. The ruins include a tower, chapel and two vaulted pit-prisons.

Halangy Down Ancient Village *see* BANT'S CARN BURIAL CHAMBER.

Halesowen Abbey (Halesowen, Birmingham)

The remains of this 13th-century abbey founded by King John have now been incorporated into a 19th-century farm.

Hallforest Castle (near Inverurie, *Aberdeenshire*)

This ruined 14th-century fortress was once the residence of the Keith family, the Earls of Kintore.

Halliggye Fogou (near Helston, *Cornwall*)

This is one of several underground tunnels, associated with Iron Age villages, found only in Cornwall.

Ham House (Richmond upon Thames, London)

This outstanding Stuart mansion was built on the banks of the Thames in 1610 and was enlarged in the 1670s. It was the centre of Carolean court life and intrigue in the 1670s when the Duke of Lauderdale, one of Charles II's most powerful ministers, married Elizabeth, Countess of Dysart.

Hampton Court Palace (near Richmond upon Thames, London)

This red-brick Tudor palace was built by Cardinal Wolsey and handed to Henry VII after its completion in 1520. In 1689 William III commissioned Christopher Wren to create extensions to the palace.

Hardknott Roman Fort (near Ravenglass, *Cumbria*)

This is one of the most dramatic Roman sites in Britain. The fort was built between AD 120 and 138 and controlled the road from Ravenglass to Ambleside. The visible remains include granaries, the building's headquarters and the commandant's house, with a bath house and parade ground outside the fort.

Hare Hill (near Lanercost, *Northumberland*)

This short section of HADRIAN'S WALL stands 2.75 metres (9 feet) high.

Harlech Castle (Harlech, *Gwynedd*)

This castle was built for Edward I between 1283 and 1289. It was built to a concentric plan on a rocky crag with the sea on one side and a moat on the other. It was seized by Owain Glyndwr and was held by him for four years. It was a Lancastrian stronghold in the Wars of the Roses and a Royalist one in the Civil War, earning it the name of 'Castle of Lost Causes'.

Harrow's Scar Milecastle (near Greenhead, *Northumberland*)

The remains are linked to BIRDOSWALD FORT by what is probably the most instructive mile section on the whole length of HADRIAN'S WALL.

Harry Avery's Castle (Newtonstewart, *County Tyrone*)

This 14th-century Gaelic stone castle was built by one of the O'Neill chiefs and is the oldest surviving Irish-built castle in Northern Ireland. The castle is in ruins and all that remains are the great twin towers of the gatehouse.

Harry's Walls (St Mary's, *Isles of Scilly*)

This 16th-century fort was intended to command the harbour of St Mary's Pool but was never completed.

Harryville Motte (Ballymena, *County Antrim*)

This Norman fort with its rectangular motte and bailey standing 12-metre (40 feet) high is one of the finest examples of Norman earthworks in Northern Ireland.

Hartland Abbey (near Hartland, *Devon*)

This 12th-century monastery was greatly added to over the course of time and was given to William Abbott in 1546 by Henry VIII. It is still owned by that family and is used as a private home.

Haseley Manor (near Newport, *Isle of Wight*])

This was built in the 11th century as the royal residence of King Harold.

Hatchlands Park (Guildford, *Surrey*)

This handsome brick house was built by Stiff Leadbetter in the 1750s for Admiral Boscawen, hero of the Battle of Louisburg in 1758. Robert Adam was responsible for the interior decoration.

Hatfield Earthworks (near Devizes, *Wiltshire*)

At this site, part of a Neolithic enclosure thought to be 3500 years old can be seen. At one time there was a Bronze Age barrow at the centre of the enclosure.

Hathersage (Hathersage, *Derbyshire*)

Little John of Robin Hood fame is said to be buried in the churchyard here.

Haughmond Abbey (near Shrewsbury, *Shropshire*)

The chapterhouse with its late medieval timber ceiling is of particular note at the extensive remains of this 12th-century Augustinian abbey. There are also some interesting medieval sculptures to can be seen.

Haverfordwest Castle (Haverfordwest, *Pembrokeshire*)

This ruined 12th-century castle has served many uses, including that of jail, police headquarters and museum.

Hawford Dovecote (Hawford, *Hereford and Worcester*)

This is a 16th-century half-timbered dovecote.

Hawkshead Courthouse (Hawkshead, *Cumbria*)

Dating from the 15th century, the Courthouse is all that re-

mains of the memorial buildings of Hawkshead that were once
held by Furness Abbey

Heavenfield (near Hexham, *Northumberland*)

In AD 634 King Oswald of Northumbria is said to have erected
a wooden cross on this site before he defeated Welsh and
Mercian invaders. The Church of St Oswald was built on the
site in 1737. The actual battlefield lies 2 miles (3 kilometres)
to the east of Chollerton and is marked by a tall wooden cross.

Heddon-on-the-Wall (near Heddon, *Northumberland*)

This stretch of HADRIAN'S WALL measures 3 metres (10 feet
thick) and has the remains of a medieval kiln near the west
end.

Helmsley Castle (Helmsley, *North Yorkshire*)

This 12th-century castle has spectacular earthworks surrounding the great ruined Norman keep.

Herefordshire Beacon (near Ledbury, *Hereford and Worcester*)

This isolated Iron Age fort is known as British Camp, and it is
thought that 2000 people lived here in ancient times.

Heritage Farm Park *see* BALLYMONEY HERITAGE FARM PARK.

Hermitage Castle (Liddesdale, *Scottish Borders*)

This 14th-century ruin was once closely linked to Mary Queen
of Scots, the de Soulis family and the Douglases. The castle
was largely restored in the 19th century.

Hever Castle (near Chiddingstone, *Kent*)

This was the 13th-century childhood home of Anne Boleyn.
She later married Henry VIII, who had her executed.

Hexham Abbey (Hexham, *Northumberland*)

This was built in the 12th and 13th centuries over the crypt of
an abbey built by St Wilfrid in AD 674. The abbey was built
using stone taken from the Roman camp of Corstopitum.
There is a stone seat in the choir that is known as Wilfrid's
Throne.

Hezlett House (Coleraine, *County Londonderry*)

This low thatched cottage was built around 1690 and has an interesting cruck truss roof.

High Bridestones and Flat Howe (near Whitby, *North Yorkshire*)

High Bridestones are the Bronze Age remains of two standing stone circles. Lying to the east, Flat Howe is a round Bronze Age barrow or burial mound.

Hill Hall (near Epping, *Essex*)

In this fine Elizabethan mansion it is possible to see examples of some of the earliest Renaissance decoration in the country.

Hill O' Many Stanes (Mid Clyth, *Highland*)

At this site there are more than twenty-two rows of small stones forming a fan-like formation. It is believed that the stones may have been arranged in this pattern for astronomical purposes.

Hill of Barra (near Inverurie, *Aberdeenshire*)

This is the site of the Battle of Barra, which was fought between Robert the Bruce and John Comyn in 1307. There is a Pictish fort on the hill in which Comyn is supposed to have camped.

Hillsborough Fort (Hillsborough, *County Down*)

This fort was built in 1650 by Colonel Arthur Hill on a site that had been important since early Christian times.

HMS Victory (Portsmouth, *Hampshire*)

This was Admiral Lord Nelson's flagship, and there is a plaque that marks the place where he fell during the Battle of Trafalgar in 1805.

Hoar Stone Chambered Barrow (Enstone, *Oxfordshire*)

This is a Neolithic burial chamber.

Hob Hurst's House (near Chesterfield, *Derbyshire*)

This square prehistoric burial mound has an earthwork ditch and an outer bank.

Holdenby House (near Northampton, *Northamptonshire*)
Charles I was held prisoner here after his defeat at the Battle of
Naseby in 1645.

Holm of Papa Chambered Cairn (off Papa Westray, *Orkney*)
A massive megalithic tomb can be found on this tiny island.
The tomb has a long, narrow chamber over 23 metres (75 feet)
long and fourteen beehive cells opening into the walls. There
are no indications that the island has been inhabited since the
tomb was built.

Holy Island (*Northumberland*) *see* LINDISFARNE.

Holy Island (off Arran, *North Ayrshire*)
The cave on this island is thought to have been home to St
Molaise, who died in AD 639 when he chose to take thirty dis-
eases at one time in order to avoid Purgatory. The caves also
bear runic inscriptions that can still be seen.

Holy Sepulchre, Church of the (Thetford, *Norfolk*)
The only surviving remains of the order of the Canons of the
Holy Sepulchre can be seen at this site. It is possible to see the
ruined nave of the priory church.

Holyrood Abbey (City of Edinburgh)
The Chapel Royal of Holyroodhouse was founded in 1128 by
David I of Scotland and was built for Augustinian canons. The
chapel's vaults contain the remains of Scottish monarchs.

Holyroodhouse *see* PALACE of Holyroodhouse.

Holyrood Park (City of Edinburgh)
A royal park since the early 12th century, this has been the site
of many archaelogical discoveries, including the remains of
four hill forts, settlements and evidence of prehistoric and
early medieval farming activity.

Honnington Camp (near Grantham, *Lincolnshire*)
The earthworks of this Iron Age hillfort lie on the slopes of
Ancaster Gap.

Horne's Palace *see* APPLEDORE.

Horton Court (Horton, *South Gloucestershire*)
The 12th-century Norman hall and detached late Perpendicular ambulatory of a limestone house with early Renaisance features can be seen at this site.

Hound Tor Deserted Medieval Village (near Manaton, *Devon*)
At this Dartmoor site it is possible to see the remains of three or four medieval farmsteads that are believed to date from the Bronze Age.

Houses of Parliament (Westminster, London)
This was originally the site of the principal royal residence from the time of Edward the Confessor to Henry VIII. The present buildings were constructed between 1840 and 1860.

Housesteads Roman Fort (Bardon Mill, *Northumberland*)
This is the best-preserved Roman fort in Britain. It is one of the twelve permanent forts built by Hadrian in AD 124 between milecastles 36 and 37 of HADRIAN'S WALL. The visible remains include four gates, towers, curtain walls, officer's quarters, barracks, granaries, latrines and hospital. Standing sections of the Wall run to the east of the fort.

Howden Minster (Howden, *East Riding of Yorkshire*)
This large, cathedral-like church dates from the 14th century and belonged to the Bishop of Durham.

Huntingdon (Huntingdon, *Cambridgeshire*)
Oliver Cromwell was born here in 1599, and the grammar school he attended (as did Samuel Pepys) is now a museum.

Huntingtower Castle (near Perth, *Perth and Kinross*)
At this site it is possible to see the remains of a castelled mansion consisting of two medieval towers linked by a 17th-century range.

Huntly Castle (Huntly, *Aberdeenshire*)
This ruined castle shows evidence of a 12th-century motte and

a 16th-century palace block that was built by the Gordon family.

Hurler's Stone Circles (near Minions, *Cornwall*)

These three Bronze Age stone circles standing in a line are thought to be the best examples of ceremonial standing stones in the southwest England.

Hust Castle (near Keyhaven, *Hampshire*)

This was one of the most sophisticated fortresses built by Henry VIII.

Hylton Castle (near Sunderland, *Tyne and Wear*)

This 15th-century keep-gatehouse has a fine display of medieval heraldry adorning the facades.

I

Ightham Mote (Ivy Hatch, Sevenoaks, *Kent*)

This attractive medieval moated manor house is noted for its Great Hall, Old Chapel and crypt and is thought to date from 1340. The chapel has a painted ceiling dating from the early 16th century. The drawing room has a Jacobean fireplace, frieze and 18th-century Palladian window.

Inch Abbey (Downpatrick, *County Down*)

This Cistercian abbey was founded in 1180 by John de Courcy. The abbey is now in ruins but is noted for its tall, pointed triple east window.

Inchcolm Abbey (opposite Aberdour, *Fife*)

Inchcolm island in the Firth of Forth has the best-preserved group of monastic buildings in Scotland. The abbey was founded in 1123 and also includes a 13th-century octagonal chapterhouse.

Inchmahome Priory (near Aberfoyle, *Stirling*)

The Augustinian monastery on the island of Inchmahome in

the Lake of Menteith was founded in 1238, and much of the original building remains intact.

Inchtuthil (near Dunkeld, *Perth and Kinross*)

At this site are remains of ramparts and ditches of a timber fortress built in AD 83 by the Roman general Agricola.

Innerpeffray (near Crieff, *Perth and Kinross*)

This is the home of Scotland's first public library, which was founded in 1691. The nearby church, Innerpeffray Chapel, dates from 1508.

Innisidgen Lower and Upper Burial Chambers (St Mary's, *Isles of Scilly*)

These two Bronze Age cairns stand approximately 60 metres (200 feet) apart and boast stunning views towards St Martins

Inverary (Inverary, *Argyll and Bute*)

This was the hereditary seat of the Dukes of Argyll. It was ruled by Campbell chiefs from 1400.

Invergarry Castle (Loch Oich, *Highland*)

This former MacDonnell stronghold was destroyed by the Duke of Cumberland because Bonnie Prince Charlie stayed here before and after Culloden. The Well of Seven Heads lies 1 mile (1.6 kilometres) to the south and was erected by Alaister MacDonnell in 1812 in memory of the revenge taken on the seven murderers of his clan.

Inverlochy Castle (near Fort William, *Highland*)

This is the well-preserved 13th-century castle that belonged to the Comyn family. The castle takes the form of a square with round towers at the corners. It is one of Scotland's earliest stone castles.

Inverurie (near Aberdeen, *Aberdeenshire*)

The town cemetery houses a 15-metre (50-foot) mound, the Bass, which was the site of a Norman castle. BRANDSBUTT STONE, which bears Pictish symbols, can also be seen.

Iona Abbey (Iona, off Mull, *Argyll and Bute*)

This island is a very important Christian historical site with abbey, 15th-century cathedral, ruined nunnery, St Oran's chapel and graveyard. It is the burial place of 48 Scottish kings. The abbey that can be seen today dates from the 13th century and was restored in the mid-20th century. The oldest remaining relic is the 4.25-metre (14-foot) high, carved St Martin's Cross, which dates from the 10th century. St Columba built a monastery on Iona in 563.

Iron Bridge (Ironbridge, *Shropshire*)

This is Britain's most famous industrial monument and is the world's first iron bridge. It was erected across the River Severn in 1779.

Isle of Whithorn (near Whithorn, *Dumfries and Galloway*)

St Ninian landed here in AD 395 on return from Rome. Today it is possible to see the remains of an Iron Age fort and the ruins of a 13th-century chapel.

Isleham Priory Church (Isleham, *Cambridgeshire*)

This rare example of an early Norman church has undergone few alterations despite being converted into a barn.

Ivinghoe Beacon (near Luton, *Bedfordshire*)

This was one of several beacon points established during the reign of Elizabeth I. The beacons were intended to summon men in case of a Spanish invasion.

J

Jacob's Well (City of Bristol)

The oldest Hebrew inscriptions found in Britain were discovered at the site of this well dating from 1042. It was used to fill the ritual bath of the local Jewish community.

Jarlshof (Sumburgh Head, *Shetland*)

This remarkable archaeological site is very important, with a complex of ancient settlements within three acres. The oldest settlement is a village of Bronze Age stone huts. Above this is an Iron Age broch and wheelhouses, and above that are stone rectangular houses that remain from a Viking community. A ruined 17th-century house is on the crest of the mound.

Jedburgh Abbey (Jedburgh, *Scottish Borders*)

This church, founded in 1138 by David I, is still remarkably complete. It is mostly built in Romanesque and early Gothic styles. The remains include the recently uncovered cloister buildings where several finds were made, including the 12th-century 'Jedburgh comb'.

Jervaulx Abbey (near Leyburn, *North Yorkshire*)

This now ruined 12th-century Cistercian foundation once had an abbot who was executed for taking part in an unsuccessful revolt against Henry VIII.

Jewel Tower (Westminster, London)

This is one of the two surviving buildings of the original Palace of Westminster. Built in 1365 to house the treasure of Edward III, it was later used as government offices and as a store.

Jewry Wall (Leicester, *Leicestershire*)

This is one of the largest surviving stretches of Roman wall in Britain. Standing over 9 metres (30 feet) high, it formed one side of the civic bath's exercise hall.

John Knox House (City of Edinburgh)

This house on Edinburgh's Royal Mile is associated with Scotland's religious reformer, John Knox, who is said to have preached to crowds from this house's window.

Jordan Hill Roman Temple (Weymouth, *Dorset*)

At this site are the foundations of a Romano-Celtic temple that enclose an area of 22 square metres (240 square feet).

Jordan's Castle (Ardglass, *County Down*)

In the 14th and 15th centuries a ring of tower houses and fortified warehouses was built to protect the port of Ardglass which was the busiest seaport in Northern Ireland. Jordan's Castle is a 15th-century four-storey tower house that stands in the town centre. It was besieged in the early 17th century and was held for three years.

Jorvik (York, *North Yorkshire*)

This Viking city was founded in AD 867. Relics from excavations of the site have been used to build reconstructions of Viking life at the Jorvik Viking Centre.

K

Kedleston Hall (Derby, *Derbyshire*)

This mansion was built between 1759 and 1765 for Nathaniel Curzon, first Baron Scarsdale, whose family had lived at Kedleston since the 12th century. It houses the most complete and least altered sequence of Robert Adam interiors in England.

Kellie Castle (near Pittenweem, *Fife*)

This is a fine example of the domestic architecture of Lowland Scotland. The oldest part of the castle is thought to date from 1360, but the majority of the building dates from the late 16th and early 17th centuries.

Kellis Chapel (near Tayvallich, *Argyll and Bute*)

This small West Highland chapel houses a collection of West Highland grave slabs and Kellis Cross.

Kelso Abbey (Kelso, *Scottish Borders*)

This abbey, which is now in ruins, was founded in 1128 by Benedictine monks from Chartres in France who were brought to Kelso by David I.

Kel Stone *see* CAIY STONE.

Kemp's Castle *see* TURIN HILL.

Kendal (Kendal, *Cumbria*)

The ruined 12th-century castle here was the birthplace of Catherine Parr in 1512. Catherine Parr was the last wife of Henry VIII.

Kenilworth Castle (Kenilworth, *Warwickshire*)

The castle was begun in the 12th century and the red sandstone keep dates from this period. The castle was eventually passed on to John of Gaunt who made it into a splendid fortified home. It was then used as a royal residence by his son, Henry IV, and it continued to be used as such until 1563. In 1563 Elizabeth I gave the castle along with the title of earl of Leicester to Robert Dudley. Under Dudley's reign Kenilworth became a fashionable playground but slid into decay after his death, accelerated by the attentions of Cromwell's troops.

Kensington Palace (Kensington, London)

This was a country house when it was bought by William III in 1689 as a royal residence. Additions were made by Sir Christopher Wren.

Kent's Cavern (near Torquay, *Devon*)

These caves were inhabited by primitive man 250,000 years ago.

Kidalton Cross (Islay, *Argyll and Bute*)

This 9th/10th-century High Cross is the finest surviving example of its type in Scotland.

Kidwelly Castle (Kidwelly, *Carmarthenshire*)

This castle was originally a huge earthwork established in the 12th century. A stone castle was built by the de Chaworths during the 13th century, and this was later modified by the Earls of Lancaster. The remains that can be seen today are still impressive.

Kilberry Sculptured Stones (near Lochgilphead, *Argyll and Bute*)

This collection of late medieval sculptured stones was gathered from the Kilberry estate.

Kilchattan (Colonsay, *Argyll and Bute*)

The remains of a medieval church that is thought to have been dedicated to St Catan can be found within a walled burial ground at this site in the southern Inner Hebrides.

Kilchurn Castle (Loch Awe, *Argyll and Bute*)

This square tower was built in the mid-16th century by Sir Colin Campbell of Glenorchy. Although now in ruins, it was enlarged in 1693 to create its present picturesque outline.

Kildrummy Castle (near Alford, *Aberdeenshire*)

This 13th-century castle, although ruined, is a fine example with its curtain wall, four round towers, hall and chapel. It was the seat of the Earl of Mar and was dismantled in 1715 after the first Jacobite uprising.

Killevy Churches (Camlough, *County Armagh*)

There are the ruins of two churches standing back to back at this site. One dates from the 10th century and the other from the 13th. They stand on the site of an important nunnery founded in the 5th century by St Monenna. In the graveyard there is a large granite slab that is said to mark St Monenna's grave. The nunnery was in use up until the time of the dissolution of the monasteries in 1542.

Killiecrankie (Killiecrankie, *Perth and Kinross*)

In 1689 the first shots in the Jacobite cause were fired here as this was the first attempt by the Jacobites to restore the exiled King James II and VII. The Jacobites were victorious in the Battle of Killiecrankie, and the Government troops were overwhelmed by the wild charge of Highland clans. However, the Jacobite leader, John Graham of Claverhouse, Viscount Dundee, was killed by a stray bullet at the battle, and without his leadership the rebellion collapsed. Soldier's Leap is a famous spot at Killiecrankie where one government soldier, Donald MacBean, leapt 6 metres (20 feet) across River Garry to avoid being slain by the Highland army.

Kilmartin Sculptured Stones (Kilmartin, *Argyll and Bute*)

In Kilmartin churchyard there are more than 24 carved West Highland grave slabs.

Kilmichael Glassary Cup and Ring Marks (Kilmichael Glassary, *Argyll and Bute*)

At this site there are Bronze Age cup and ring marks carved on a natural rock outcrop.

Kilmodan Sculptured Stones (Clachan of Glendaruel, *Argyll and Bute*)

A group of West Highland carved grave slabs lie in the churchyard at this site.

Kilmory Knap Chapel (Kilmory, South Knapdale, *Argyll and Bute*)

This small, medieval West Highland church has a collection of West Highland grave slabs and in the graveyard it has Macmillan's Cross, a fine example of medieval carving.

Kilnasaggart (Jonesborough, *County Armagh*)

This granite pillar stone dates back to the 8th century and is carved with numerous crosses and a long Irish inscription.

Kilphedir (near Helmsdale, *Highland*)

This Iron Age broch has a 10-metre (32-foot) diameter and is enclosed by 4.5-metre (15-foot) thick walls. Around the tower are stone circles that show sites of huts, and there is an underground passage or earth house. The outer enclosure is protected by bank and ditches.

Kilwinning Abbey (Kilwinning, *North Ayrshire*)

Little remains of this Tironensian-Benedictine abbey. The remaining fragments appear to date from the 13th century and include part of the abbey church and the chapterhouse.

Kimbolton (Kimbolton, *Cambridgeshire*)

The village has a Tudor manor that was remodelled in 1707. Catherine of Aragon was imprisoned in the castle here after being divorced by Henry VIII.

King Charles's Castle (Tresco, *Isles of Scilly*)

This was built in the 1550s for coastal defence but was badly designed and was superseded in 1651 by CROMWELL'S CASTLE.

King Charles's Tower (Chester, *Cheshire*)

King Charles I is said to have stood here in 1645 to watch his troops being defeated on Rowtown Moor

King Doniert's Stone (St Cleer, *Cornwall*)

Two pieces of a 9th-century decorated cross can be seen at this site. The cross has an inscription thought to commemorate Durngrath, king of Cornwall, who drowned in about 875.

King James's and Landport Gates (Portsmouth, *Hampshire*)

These two gates once formed part of the 17th-century defences of Portsmouth.

King's Bath *see* ROMAN BATHS.

King's College Chapel (Cambridge, *Cambridgeshire*)

This Gothic masterpiece was begun in 1446 under the instruction of Henry VI. It was completed in 1515 by Henry VIII.

King's Head (Aylesbury, *Buckinghamshire*)

This coaching inn dates from 1450. The large window in the parlour contains fragments of 15th-century glass and shows figures of angels holding shields, some of which bear the arms of Henry VI and his wife, Margaret of Anjou.

King's Men, The *see* ROLLRIGHT STONES.

King's Sedge Moor (near Glastonbury, *Somerset*)

The Battle of Sedgemoor, the last battle on English soil, was fought here in 1685. Monmouth's rebels were defeated by the forces of James II.

King Stone, The *see* ROLLRIGHT STONES.

Kingston Russell Stone Circle (near Abbotsbury, *Dorset*)
This Bronze Age stone circle consists of eighteen stones.

Kingswood Abbey Gatehouse (Kingswood, *Gloucestershire*)
This 16th-century gatehouse is all that remains of the Cistercian abbey.

Kinlochaline Castle (near Lochaline, *Highland*)
This 14th-century tower house was restored in 1890. There is a fireplace on the roof that is said to have been used to heat oil and water to pour on attackers.

Kinnaird Head Lighthouse (Fraserburgh, *Aberdeenshire*)
This 16th-century castle was built for the Fraser family and was adapted to take the first lighthouse built by the Northern Lighthouse Company in 1787.

Kinwarton Dovecote (Kinwarton, *Warwickshire*)
This circular 14th-century dovecote has a fine ogee doorway and retains its potence—a rare feature.

Kirby Muxloe Castle (near Leicester, *Leicestershire*)
This picturesque, moated brick castle was founded in 1480 by William, Lord Hastings.

Kirk Dale (near Helmsley, *North Yorkshire*)
The remains of a prehistoric mammoth, lion and hippopotamus were found in a cave here in 1821.

Kirkham Priory (near Malton, *North Yorkshire*)
The ruins of this Augustinian priory include a splendid carved gatehouse.

Kirkmadrine Early Christian Stones (near Stranraer, *Dumfries and Galloway*)
Displayed in the porch of a former chapel in the Rinns of Galloway, these are three of the earliest Christian memorial stones in Britain, dating from the 5th and 6th centuries.

Kirk Yetholm (near Kelso, *Scottish Borders*)
This is where gypsy queens were crowned until the 19th century.

Kit's Coty House and Little Kit's Coty House (near Maidstone, *Kent*)

At this site it is possible to see the remains of two prehistoric burial chambers. They take their names from the Celtic phrase meaning 'tomb in the woods'.

Knap of Howar (Papa Westray, *Orkney*)

This group of standing stone houses are probably the oldest in northwest Europe, dating from the early Neolithic period. There are two houses, which are approximately rectangular in shape with stone cupboards and stalls.

Knights Templar Church (Dover, *Kent*)

The foundations of this small, circular 12th-century church stand across the valley from Dover Castle.

Knock Castle (near Ballater, *Aberdeenshire*)

A bare keep is all that remains of this late 16th-century stronghold that once belonged to the Gordon family who were gruesomely murdered in the 16th century.

Knock Castle (Skye, *Highland*)

This is one of the many strongholds that belonged to the MacDonald clan in the 16th and 17th centuries. This castle was successfully defended against an attack by the Clan McLeod in the 15th century.

Knowe of Yarso Chambered Cairn (Rousay, *Orkney*)

Dating from Neolithic times, this is an oval cairn with concentric walls enclosing a chambered tomb that is divided into three compartments.

Knowlton Church and Earthworks (near Cranborne, *Dorset*)

Standing in the middle of Neolithic earthworks, this ruined Norman church symbolizes the transition from pagan to Christian worship.

L

Lacock Abbey (Lacock, *Wiltshire*)

This abbey was founded in 1232 and was converted into a manor house after 1539. The medieval cloisters, sacristy and chapterhouse are of particular interest, as are the 16th-century stable and the 18th-century Gothic hall.

Ladykirk (near Swinton, *Scottish Borders*)

This pale pink church with its three-storey tower and fine carvings was built in gratitude by James IV after he was saved from drowning in the River Tweed.

Laggangairn Standing Stones (Killgallioch, *Dumfries and Galloway*)

After gaining access through Forestry Commission Land, it is possible to see two stones carved with early Christian crosses.

Lambeth Palace (Westminster, *London*)

This has been the official home of the Archbishop of Canterbury since the 13th century. The Tudor gateway dates from 1495 and the Great Hall from 1660. Parts of the Chapel date from the early 13th century.

Lamphey Palace (Lamphey, *Pembrokeshire*)

This ruined 13th-century palace once belonged to the Bishops of St David's.

Lancaster Castle (Lancaster, *Lancashire*)

This stands on a medieval site but was largely rebuilt in the 18th century.

Landguard Fort (Felixstowe, *Suffolk*)

This was an 18th-century fort that was altered by later additions.

Lanercost Priory (near Brampton, *Cumbria*)

This Augustinian priory was founded in 1166 and was damaged in the 13th and 14th centuries by Scottish invaders. It
was abandoned in 1536 during the dissolution of the monasteries. The surviving remains include the north aisle, the ruined chancel, transepts and priory buildings.

Langcliffe Scar (near Settle, *North Yorkshire*)

The headlands of the scar are riddled with caves. Remains of
Ice Age animals and Stone Age, Roman and Celtic artefacts
have all been excavated at Victoria Cave.

Langley Chapel (near Acton Burrell, *Shropshire*)

This small chapel contains a complete set of early 17th-cen-
tury wooden fittings and furniture.

Largs Old Kirk (Largs, *North Ayrshire*)

This monument was erected in 1636 as an addition to the parish church. It contains an elaborately carved stone tomb in the
Renaissance style and a painted ceiling that illustrates the sea-
sons.

Laugharne Castle (Laugharne, *Carmarthenshire*)

This castle was originally established during the 12th century
but was transformed by a series of occupiers, including the
Anglo-Norman de Brian family and Sir John Perrot.

Launceston Castle (Launceston, *Cornwall*)

This medieval castle, set on the motte of a Norman castle, controlled the main route into Cornwall. Today the shell keep and
tower survive.

Leahill Turret and Piper Sike Turret (near Brampton, *Cumbria*)

These turrets can be found in the section of HADRIAN'S WALL
to the west of BIRDOSWALD FORT. They were originally constructed for the turf wall.

Legananny Dolmen (Dromara, *County Down*)

This is one of the most splendid Stone Age monuments in

Northern Ireland. It is a tripod dolmen which has three tall up-rights and a huge capstone.

Leicester's Church see DENBIGH TOWN WALLS.

Leigh Barton (near Kingsbridge, *Devon*)

This small late medieval domestic complex has a fine gate-house and three ranges around a galleried court.

Leigh Court Barn (near Worcester, *Hereford and Worcester*)

This splendid 14th-century timber-framed barn was built for the monks of Pershore Abbey. It is the largest of its kind in Britain.

Leiston Abbey (near Leiston, *Surrey*)

This was an abbey for Premonstratensian canons, originally founded in the 12th century. The remains include a restored chapel.

Lexden Earthworks and Bluebottle Grove (Colchester, *Essex*)

At this site parts of earthworks, which once covered 31 square kilometres (12 square miles), can be seen. These earthworks were built to protect Iron Age Colchester and were subse-quently added to by the conquering Romans.

Lilleshall Abbey (near Oakengates, *Shropshire*)

The ruins of this abbey of Augustinian canons include the re-mains of the 12th- and 13th-century church and the cloister.

Lincluden Collegiate Church (Dumfries, *Dumfries and Galloway*)

The remains of a collegiate church and the accommodation for its canons can be seen at this site. The church was founded in 1389 by Archibald the Grim, the third Earl of Douglas. The church has a splendid chancel, thought to have been added by Archibald, the fourth Earl, and this houses the exquisite tomb of his wife, Princess Margaret, daughter of Robert III.

Lincoln Bishop's Old Palace (Lincoln, *Lincolnshire*)

The remains of this medieval palace of the Bishops of Lincoln include Alnwick Tower.

Lincoln Castle (Lincoln, *Lincolnshire*)

This castle was built in 1068 by William the Conqueror, and in the early 13th century it was a focal point for the struggle between King John and his barons. It is now home to the Magna Carta.

Lincoln Cathedral (Lincoln, *Lincolnshire*)

The cathedral was first begun in 1072 by Bishop Remigius. His church was destroyed by an earthquake in 1185 and Bishop Hugh began its reconstruction in 1192. The central tower was constructed between 1307 and 1311.

Lindisfarne *or* Holy Island (*Northumberland*)

The island of Lindisfarne has an illustrious history. St Aidan of Iona founded a monastery here in 635 at the invitation of King Oswald of Northumbria. The northeast was soon evangelized by the monks, who established a reputation for scholarship.

The monastery had sixteen bishops in total, the most celebrated being St Cuthbert, who was pleaded with to take the post by Ecgfrith, another Northumbrian king. St Cuthbert could not settle at Lindisfarne and within two years he had returned to his hermetic cell on the Farne Islands, where he died in 687. After his death, his body was taken back to Lindisfarne to be buried. Lindisfarne became a shrine when, 11 years after his burial, St Cuthbert was dug up and found to be undecayed. Lindisfarne became a place of pilgrimage until 875 when the monks fled the island in fear of the plundering Vikings. The monks took St Cuthbert's remains with them and they now rest at Durham Cathedral.

In 1082 Lindisfarne was renamed Holy Island and was colonized by Benedictine monks from Durham who re-established a religious house on the island. The last of the monks were evicted in 1537 during the dissolution of the monasteries.

Lindisfarne priory is situated near the centre of the village, and the pink sandstone ruins of the church from the Benedictine foundation remain, giving a clear indication of the original structure of the priory. Of particular note are the tight Romanesque arches of the nave and the impressive stonework of the central tower's last remaining arch. Behind the monastic remains is the 13th-century church of St Mary the Virgin.

Lindisfarne Castle was built in the 16th century to defend the island's harbour from the Scots. It was transformed into a holiday home by Sir Edward Lutyens in 1901.

Linlithgow Palace (Linlithgow, *West Lothian*)

This great royal palace is now in ruins but is still set in its own park beside Linlithgow Loch. It was a favourite residence of the Stewart royalty from James I (1406-37) on. Today it is still possible to see works that were commissioned by James I, III, IV, V and VI. Both James V and Mary Queen of Scots were born here. The palace was burned by Hanoverian troops during the final Jacobite rebellion in 1745.

Little Dean Hall (near Gloucester, *Gloucestershire*)

This is believed to be Britain's oldest inhabited house. The only known remains of a Saxon hall can be seen in the basement and there is a Roman temple in the grounds.

Little Moreton Hall (Congleton, *Cheshire*)

This is regarded as the finest example of a timber-framed moated manor house in Britain. It was begun in 1450 and was finally completed in 1580. Of particular interest are the chapel, Elizabethan Long Gallery, Great Hall, wall paintings and the Knot Garden.

Liverpool Playhouse (Liverpool, *Merseyside*)

This is Britain's oldest working repertory theatre.

Llanaelhaern (Llanaelhaern, *Gwynedd*)

The village church is dedicated to Aelhaern, the 6th-century saint, and the churchyard contains Celtic headstones.

Llandaff Cathedral (Llandaff, *Cardiff*)

Built on the site of a church founded in the 6th century and made of wood, this cathedral was built from Norman stone in the 12th century but subsequently largely rebuilt.

Llanddewi-Brefi (Llanddewi-Brefi, *Ceredigion*)

In AD 519 St David is said to have addressed a turbulent meeting here and according to legend the ground rose up beneath his feet. The Church of St David stands on the site of the meeting place.

Llanegan (Llanegan, *Gwynedd*)

The original village church was founded in the 6th century by St Einion, king of Lleyn. The present church dates from the 15th century and has a double nave and a 16th-century tower.

Llangar Church *see* RHUG CHAPEL.

Llanstephan Castle (Llanstephan, *Carmarthenshire*)

The ruins of this stronghold date from the 11th to 13th centuries.

Llanthony Priory (Llanthony, *Monmouthshire*)

The remains of a 6th-century hermitage dedicated to St David were the site for this priory, which was founded by William Lacey in the early 12th century. By 1108 a church had been consecrated on the site, and ten years later the priory was completed. In 1135 the priory was brought to a state of siege, and in 1175 Hugh de Lacey founded a new church. It is the ruined remains of this church that can be seen today. The remains include the west towers, north nave arcade and south transept.

Llantwit Major (Llantwit Major, *Vale of Glamorgan*)

St Illtyd founded a monastery here in the 5th century. Today a church stands on this site, and it has a thousand-year-old stone font.

Llawhaden Castle (Llawhaden, *Pembrokeshire*)

This castle was first built in the 12th century to protect the possessions of the bishops of St Davids. The remains of the bishop's hall, bakehouse and other buildings added in the 13th and 14th centuries can all be seen.

Llywernog Silver-Lead Mines (Ponterwyd, *Ceredigion*)
The tunnels and chambers of this mine date from the 18th century. The old mine buildings at the surface have been refurbished and contain exhibitions on the mines.

Loanhead Stone Circle (near Daviot, *Aberdeenshire*)
This is the best known of a group of recumbent stone circles enclosing a stone cairn. Beside the stone circle there is a small burial enclosure that is thought to be 4000–5000 years old.

Lochleven Castle (Loch Leven, *Perth and Kinross*)
In 1567 Mary Queen of Scots was imprisoned in this late 14th-century tower. She later made her escape from the island, in 1568.

Lochmaben Castle (near Lochmaben, *Dumfries and Galloway*)
This royal castle by Castle Loch was originally built by the English in the 14th century but was extensively rebuilt in 1588 under the reign of James IV. Today only greatly reduced remains can be seen.

Lochnan Uamh (near Arisaig, *Highland*)
This broad bay is where Bonnie Prince Charlie landed on 25 July 1745 and where he left for France the following year after the Jacobites' defeat at Culloden. He and his followers are thought to have sheltered in the caves below Arisaig House. There is a cairn on the shore to commemorate the importance of this site.

Lochranza Castle (Isle of Arran, *North Ayrshire*)
This fine tower house is thought to date from the 16th century and is probably the reconstruction of an even earlier building.

Londonderry City Walls (Londonderry, *County Londonderry*)
These are the finest and most complete city walls to be found

in Northern Ireland. They are 6–8 metres (20–25 feet) high and mounted with an ancient canon. The walls date back to the 17th century.

London Wall (Tower Hill, London)

This part of the eastern defences of the City of London is the best-preserved piece of the Roman Wall that can be seen in London. It was heightened in the Middle Ages.

Long Crendon Courthouse (Aylesbury, *Buckinghamshire*)

This two-storey 14th-century building is partly half-timbered and is thought to have been originally used as a wool store. From the reign of Henry V until recent times, the manorial courts were held here.

Longcroft Hillfort *see* ADDINSTON AND LONGCROFT HILL FORTS.

Long Mountain (near Welshpool, *Powys*)

Henry Tudor camped here in 1485, before crossing the border to defeat Richard III at the Battle of Bosworth after which he took the English throne as Henry VI.

Longthorpe Tower (near Peterborough, *Cambridgeshire*)

This tower forms part of a fortified manor house and houses the Great Chamber, which has the best examples of domestic wall paintings in northern Europe. The paintings show many sacred and secular objects, including the Wheel of Life, the Labours of the Months, the Nativity and King David.

Longtown Castle (near Abbey Dore, *Hereford and Worcester*)

This unusual cylindrical keep was built at the start of the 13th century and has walls that are 4.5 metres (15 feet) thick.

Loudon Wood Stone Circle (near Peterhead, *Aberdeenshire*)

In a forest clearing it is possible to see Buchan prehistoric stone circle, the central stone of which weighs approximately 12 tons.

Loughinisland Churches (Downpatrick, *County Down*)

This group of three ancient churches stands on an island in the lough that is accessible by a causeway. The oldest church stands in the middle and dates back to the 13th century and has a draw-bar hole to secure the door. The large north church dates back to the 15th century and is thought to have been built to replace the middle church. It was in use up until 1720. The south church is the smallest and most recent.

Lower Brockhampton (near Bromyard, *Hereford and Worcester*)
This late 14th-century moated manor house has an attractive detached half-timbered 15th-century gatehouse and is a rare example of this type of structure. There are also the remains of a 12th-century chapel at this site.

Ludgershall Castle and Cross (Ludgershall, *Wiltshire*)
At this site lie the remains of a 12th-century royal hunting palace and a late medieval cross.

Lullingstone Roman Villa (near Eynsford, *Kent*)
This villa dates from AD 100 and was extended through 300 years of Roman occupation. Originally the villa was fronted by a verandah with projecting wings. Over the period of occupation the bath houses were extended and a large apsed dining room was added. In the cellar there is an early shrine that has frescoes of water nymphs. Later still some of the rooms were made into a chapel following the introduction of Christianity.

Lulworth Castle (Lulworth, *Dorset*)
This early 17th-century hunting lodge became a fashionable country house in the 18th century.

Lyddington Bede House (Lyddington, *Leicestershire*)
This house of prayer was originally a medieval palace of the Bishops of Lincoln. It was later converted into an almshouse.

Lydford Castle and Saxon Town (Lydford, *Devon*)
This 12th-century tower was a notorious prison and stands to the north of the earthworks at the site of the original Norman fort.

Lytes Cary Manor (Somerton, *Somerset*)

This manor house has a 14th-century chapel, a 15th-century hall and a 16th-century Great Chamber.

M

MacFie's Stone (Colonsay, *Argyll and Bute*)

This is the site in the southern Inner Hebrides of the murder of the clan chief, and many clan members visit the site. There are two carved stones that are thought to indicate that the site was an early Christian burial ground.

Machrie Moor Stone Circle (near Blackwaterfoot, Arran, *North Ayrshire*)

This is one of the most impirtant sites of its type in Britain. Here it is possible to see the remains of five Bronze Age stone circles.

Machynlleth (Machynlleth, *Gwynedd*)

A building in Maengwyn Street stands on the site of the original Welsh Parliament, which was held by the rebel leader Owain Glyndwr in 1404.

McLean's Cross (Iona, off Mull, *Argyll and Bute*)

This is a fine example of a 15th-century free-standing cross.

MacLellan's Castle (Kirkcudbright, *Dumfries and Galloway*)

This castelled town house is complete, with the exception of its roof. It was built in the 1570s by Thomas MacLellan, the then provost of Kirkcudbright, but was probably never completed.

Maes Howe Chambered Cairn (near Kirkwall, *Orkney*)

This is the finest example of a megalithic tomb in the British Isles. It has a large mound that covers a stone-built passage and also a large burial chamber that has cells in the walls. The tomb dates from the Neolithic period but was broken into by Vikings, and there are Viking runes carved on the walls

Maghera Church (Maghera, *County Londonderry*)

This parish church was originally an important monastery founded in the 6th century by St Lurach. The church has been greatly altered over the centuries but is noted for its 12th-century west door and a cross-carved stone lying to the west of the church, which is thought to be the grave of St Lurach.

Maghera Church (Newcastle, *County Down*)

The only remains of an early maonastery that once stood at this site is the stump of a round tower that was blown down in a storm in the 18th century. The remains of a 13th-century church can be found nearby.

Maiden Castle (near Dorchester, *Dorset*)

This is thought to be the finest Iron Age hillfort in Britain. It has enormous earthworks with a series of ramparts and complicated entrances. These defences did not prevent the castle from being captured by the Romans in AD 43.

Maiden Stone (near Inverurie, *Aberdeenshire*)

This Pictish cross-slab dates from the 9th century and has a Celtic cross carved on one side and Pictish symbols on the other.

Maison Dieu (Ospringe, *Kent*)

This is part of a medieval complex consisting of royal lodge, almshouses and a hospital. Today it is much as it was in the 16th century. It has a crown-post roof and a decorative ceiling.

Maison Dieu Chapel (Brechin, *Angus*)

Part of the south wall of a 13th-century chapel that was built beside a medieval hospital can be seen at thsi site.

Manorbier (Manorbier, *Pembrokeshire*)

The ruins of a moated 12th-century castle stand above Manorbier Bay. The remains of the castle include the inner court, the vast gatehouse and the hall and chapel.

Marble Hill House (Twickenham, London)

This Thames-side villa was built in 1724-29 for Henrietta Howard, Countess of Suffolk. The Great Room has lavish gilded decoration and architectural paintings by Panini.

Margam Abbey and Stones Museum (near Port Talbot, *Neath Port Talbot*)

The abbey dates from1147 and the Stones Museum contains original Celtic stone crosses dating from the 5th century

Marmion Tower (near Ripon, *North Yorkshire*)

This medieval gatehouse has a fine oriel window.

Mar's Wark (Stirling, *Stirling*)

This remarkable Renaissance mansion was built in 1570 by the Regent Mar. Today only the facade remains.

Martin's Haven (near Marloes, *Pembrokeshire*)

A Stone Age tribe built a defensive earthwork in this steep-sided valley.

Martyrs' Memorial (Oxford, *Oxfordshire*)

This Victorian Gothic memorial was erected to comemorate Bishops Latimer and Ridley who were burned at the stake in 1555 for their Protestant beliefs and to Bishop Cranmer who was similarly fated in 1556.

Mattersey Priory (near Mattersey, *Nottinghamshire*)

At this site it is possible to see the remains of a small Gilbertine monastery that was founded in 1185.

Mayburgh Earthwork (near Eamont Bridge, *Cumbria*)

This impressive, circular prehistoric earthwork encloses a central area of $1^1/_2$ acres that contains a single stone.

Meare Fish House (Meare, *Somerset*)

This is a good example of a simple stone dwelling.

Medieval Merchant's House (Southampton, *Hampshire*)

This 13th-century town house was built as a shop and home for a successful wine merchant.

Meigle Sculptured Stones (Meigle, *Angus*)

This is one of the most notable assemblages of Dark Age sculpture in Western Europe, consisting of twenty-five sculptured monuments from the early Christian period.

Melrose Abbey (Melrose, *Scottish Borders*)

This is one of the most famous ruins in Scotland. It was founded as a Cistercian abbey in 1136 by David I but was largely destroyed by the English army of Richard III in 1385. The majority of the surviving remains are of the church, dating from the 15th century, and are of an elegance unmatched in Scotland.

Memsie Cairn (near Fraserburgh, *Aberdeenshire*)

This stone-built cairn is thought to date from the Bronze Age but has been enlarged over the past two centuries.

Merchant Adventurers' Hall (York, *North Yorkshire*)

This is the finest guildhall remaining in Europe today. It has been little altered since the 14th century and houses furniture, paintings, archives, silver and other objects used by the merchants of York.

Merrivale Prehistoric Settlement (near Merrivale, *Devon*)

At this Dartmoor site two rows of standing stones stretch for 264 metres (864 feet) across the moors. The remains of an early Bronze Age village can also be seen.

Middleham Castle (Middleham, *North Yorkshire*)

This was the childhood home of Richard III. There is a huge 12th-century keep, and its battlements offer wonderful views over the surrounding countryside.

Middle Littleton Tithe Barn (Middle Littleton, *Hereford and Worcester*)

This splendid 13th-century tithe barn is built of blue lias stone.

Midhowe Chambered Cairn (Rousay, *Orkney*)

This large, impressive megalithic chambered tomb is an oval

mound and has twenty-four stalls. It dates from the Neolithic period

Milton Chantry (Gravesend, *Kent*)

This small 14th-century building once housed the chapel of a leper hospital and a family chantry. In 1780 it was incorporated into a fort.

Minster Lovell Hall and Dovecot (near Witney, *Oxfordshire*)

At this site it is possible to see the handsome remains of Lord Lovell's 15th-century manor house.

Mistley Towers (Lawford, *Essex*)

This church was built by Robert Adam in 1776. The design was unusual as it had a tower at both the west and the east end.

Mitchell's Fold Stone Circle (near Shrewsbury, *Shropshire*)

This Bronze Age stone circle consists of thirty stones, fifteen of which are visible.

Monea Castle (Enniskillen, *County Fermanagh*)

This is a fine example of a plantation castle and it still has much of its enclosing bawn wall intact. It was built around 1618 and is noted for its stone corbelling—the Scottish method of supporting the turrets.

Monk Bretton Priory (Barnsley, *South Yorkshire*)

The ruins of a Cluniac monastery founded in 1153 can be seen at this site. There are extensive remains of the 14th-century gatehouse, which has been fully restored.

Monmouth Castle (Monmouth, *Monmouthshire*)

The town's ruined castle was the birthplace of Henry V in 1387.

Montgomery (Montgomery, *Powys*)

This small town has evidence of Neolithic, Iron Age, Roman and medieval fortifications, the latter including a 13th-century castle built by Henry II on the site of a Norman motte, of which fragments of the towers and walls remain.

Monument (City of London, London)

This fluted doric column was designed by Sir Christopher Wren to commemorate the Great Fire of 1666. It was completed in 1677.

Moreton Corbet Castle (Moreton Corbet, *Shropshire*)

This is a ruined medieval castle with the substantial remains of a fine Elizabethan mansion.

Morlais Castle (near Merthyr Tydfil, *Merthyr Tydfil*)

The remains of this 13th-century castle lie beneath grass-covered mounds and rock-cut ditches. The basement has splendid vaulted arches and a central pillar.

Mortlach Church (near Dufftown, *Aberdeenshire*)

This well-preserved church was founded by St Moulag in the 6th century on an ancient site. In the churchyard there is a Pictish stone that records a Pictish victory over the Danes.

Morton Castle (near Thornhill, *Dumfries and Galloway*)

This fine late 13th-century hall house was once the stronghold of the Douglases.

Moseley Old Hall (Fordhouses, Wolverhampton, *Staffordshire*)

Charles II hid at this Elizabethan house after the Battle of Worcester in 1651.

Moss Farm Road Stone Circle (near Blackwaterfoot, Arran, *North Ayrshire*)

This stone circle surrounds the remains of a Bronze Age cairn.

Mote of Mark (Dalbeattie, *Dumfries and Galloway*)

This 5th-century Celtic hillfort is well preserved and is one of the most important archaeological sites on the Solway Firth.

Motte of Urr (Dalbeattie, *Dumfries and Galloway*)

This is the most extensive motte-and-bailey castle in Scotland and dates from the 12th century.

Moulton Packhorse Bridge (Moulton, *Suffolk*)

This medieval packhorse bridge spans the River Kennett.

Mound of Down (Downpatrick, *County Down*)

At this site there was once an Early Christian hillfort that was conquered by Anglo-Norman troops in 1177. The Anglo-Normans then built an earthwork castle on top of the hillfort.

Mount Grace Priory (near Thirsk, *North Yorkshire*)

This is the most important of England's nine Carthusian ruins, and it is the only one in Yorkshire. The priory provides a stark contrast to its more grand and worldly Cistercian counterparts. It was founded in 1398, and the Carthusian monks who lived here took a vow of silence and lived, ate and prayed alone in their two-storey cells, congregating only for services in the monastery's small church.

Mount Grace fell into decline after the Reformation, and the buildings were allowed to disintegrate until, in the 17th century, a house was built for Thomas Lascelles from the remains of the Priory guest house. The foundations of the monks' cells are still clearly visible, as are other substantial remains, including the gatehouse and the walls and tower of the priory church.

Mountjoy Castle (Stewartstown, *County Tyrone*)

This early 17th-century brick and stone fort was built for Lord Deputy Mountjoy during his campaign against Hugh O'Neill, Earl of Tyrone. The fort was captured and recaptured by the Irish and the English during the 17th century. It was also used by the armies of James II and William III. The fort is in ruins today, but remains of the four rectangular towers can be seen overlooking Lough Neagh.

Mount Sandel (Coleraine, *County Londonderry*)

This 61-metre (200-foot) oval mound is thought to have been fortified in the Iron Age and is close to the earliest known inhabited place in Ireland where relics dating back to 6650 BC have been found. The fort was a stronghold of de Courcy in the 12th century and was refortified for artillery in the 17th century.

Mount Stewart House and Temple of the Winds (Newtownards, *County Down*)

This 18th-century house was the family home of the Stewarts (who later became Marquesses of Londonderry) and was the childhood home of Lord Castlereagh, Foreign Secretary from 1812 to 1823. The architecture of the house is a combination of the work of James Wyatt, George Dance and Vitruvius Morrison, which spans a period between 1780 and 1890. The Temple of the Winds was built on the shores of Strangford Lough by James Stewart in 1782 for the first Marquess.

Mousa Broch (Mousa, *Shetland*)

This Iron Age broch tower, standing over 12 metres (40 feet) high, is one of the finest surviving examples of its type.

Moyry Castle (Newry, *County Armagh*)

This tall three-storey keep was built in 1601 by Lord Mountjoy, Queen Elizabeth's deputy, to secure the Gap of the North, which was the main route into Ulster.

Muchelney Abbey (Muchelney, *Somerset*)

The ruins of this Benedictine abbey include the well-preserved remains of the cloisters and the abbot's lodging.

Multangular Tower (York, *North Yorkshire*)

This is the most spectacular remnant of the 1st-century Roman fortress-city of Eboracum, which was later incorporated into the medieval city wall.

Muncaster Castle (near Ravenglass, *Cumbria*)

This home of the Pennington family, dating from the 13th century, was where Henry VI sought sanctuary during the War of the Roses.

Muness Castle (on Unst, *Shetland*)

This is the northernmost castle in the British Isles and has fine architectural details. It is a late 16th-century tower house that has circular towers at opposite corners

Mussenden Temple Bishop's Gate and Black Glen (Downhill, *County Londonderry*)

This 18th-century rotunda was modelled on the Temple of Vesta at Tivoli. The temple was built by Frederick Harvey, Bishop of Derry and fourth Earl of Bristol as a summer library for his cousin, who died before its completion.

Muthill Old Church and Tower (Muthill, *Perth and Kinross*)

At this site it is possible to see the interesting remains of an important medieval parish church. At the west end of the church there is a tall Romanesque tower. Much of the church dates from the 15th century.

N

Na Fir Breighe *see* NORTH UIST.

Narrow Water Castle (Warrenpoint, *County Down*)

This 16th-century battlemented tower house is surrounded by a wall and juts out into the estuary that it was built to defend.

Naseby (Naseby, *Northamptonshire*)

This was the site of the Battle of Naseby in 1645 where Cromwell won a decisive victory over Charles I.

Navan Fort (Armagh, *County Armagh*)

This is one of Europe's most important Celtic sites. It was the seat of the ancient kings of Ulster and was the setting for the legends of the mythical Cuchulainn.

Neath (*Neath Port Talbot*)

This town dates back to Roman times. It was once the Roman fort of Nidum. The town also boasts the ruins of a 12th-century Norman castle.

Neath Abbey (Neath, *Neath Port Talbot*)
  This Cistercian abbey, which is now in ruins, dates from the
  12th century with many 13th-century additions.

Needles Old Battery (West Highdown, *Isle of Wight*)
  This Victorian coastal fort was built in 1862.

Neidpath Castle (near Peebles, *Scottish Borders*)
  This turreted 14th-century stronghold on a rock high above the
  Tweed valley was converted into a home in the 17th century.

Nelson's Statue (Portsmouth, *Hampshire*)
  This statue overlooks the spot where Nelson last stood before
  setting sail for Trafalgar on HMS *Victory*.

Ness of Burgi (Scatness, *Shetland*)
  This stone-built blockhouse is thought to date from the Iron
  Age and is similar to a broch in some of its features.

Netheravon Dovecote (Netheravon, *Wiltshire*)
  This 18th-century brick dovecote still has the majority of its
  700 or more nesting boxes.

Nether Largie Cairns (near Kilmartin, *Argyll and Bute*)
  There are three cairns at this site. Two date from the Bronze
  Age and the third is from the Neolithic period (about 3000 BC).

Netley Abbey (Netley, *Hampshire*)
  In Tudor times this 13th-century Cistercian abbey was converted into a house.

Nevern (Nevern, *Pembrokeshire*)
  The village's Norman church has a carved Celtic cross and a
  'bleeding yew' that drips blood-red sap.

New Abbey Corn Mill (near Dumfries, *Dumfries and Galloway*)
  This is an 18th-century water-powered mill for making oat-
  meal that has been restored to working order.

Newark Castle (Newark-on-Trent, *Nottinghamshire*)
  King John died in 1216 in this 12th-century castle, which was
  reduced to ruins after the Civil War.

Newark Castle (Port Glasgow, *Inverclyde*)

The tower is the oldest part of the castle and dates from the mid 15th century and has a detached gatehouse. The main part of the castle was added in the late 16th century by Patrick Maxwell and has an elegant style.

Newburgh Priory (near Helmsley, *North Yorkshire*)

This 12th-century priory has been incorporated into a house. The remains of Oliver Cromwell are said to lie in a vault beneath the house.

Newcastle Castle (Bridgend, *Bridgend*)

This small, ruined castle dates from the 12th century. The remains include a rectangular tower, a carved Norman gateway and massive curtain walls enclosing a polygonal courtyard.

New Lanark (near Lanark, *South Lanarkshire*)

A model mill village set up by David Dale and Robert Owen in 1784 lies near the Falls of Clyde.

Nine Ladies Stone Circle (Stanton Moor, *Derbyshire*)

This Bronze Age circle, measuring 15 metres (50 feet) across, was once the burial site for 300–400 people.

Nine Stones, The (Winterbourne Abbas, *Dorset*)

Nine standing stones make this prehistoric stone circle, which is thought to have been constructed about 4000 years ago.

Noltland Castle (Westray, *Orkney*)

This fine Z-plan tower was built between 1560 and 1573 but was never completed. It is notable for its large number of gun loops and its impressive staircase.

Norham Castle (Norham, *Northumberland*)

This castle, built in 1160, was one of the strongest Border castles and was set on a promontory in a curve of the River Tweed.

Norman's Law (near Newburgh, *Fife*)

This complex Iron Age hillfort stands on the top of a 305-metre (1000-foot) hill. It comprises a stone wall surrounding the summit and a further wall on the lower slopes.

North Elmhalm Chapel (near East Dereham, *Norfolk*)

The remains of this Norman chapel were converted into a fortified dwelling and surrounded by earthworks in the late 14th century by Hugh le Despenser, the notorious Bishop of Norwich.

North Hinksey Conduit House (North Hinksey, *Oxfordshire*)

This is the roofed reservoir for the first water mains in Oxford. It was built at the start of the 17th century.

North Leigh Roman Villa (near North Leigh, *Oxfordshire*)

The most important feature of this large Roman courtyard villa is the almost complete mosaic tile floor, which is intricately patterned in reds and browns.

North Uist (North Uist, *Western Isles*)

This island in the Outer Hebrides is rich in ancient forts, ruins and standing stones. North of Lochmaddy is a stone group called Na Fir Breighe, 'The False Men', which legend tells us is either of wife deserters turned to stone or the gravestones of spies who were buried alive.

Northington Grange (near New Alresford, *Hampshire*)

This is a splendid example of a neoclassical country house, which was built at the beginning of the 18th century.

Notgrove Long Barrow (near Notgrove, *Gloucestershire*)

A stone-built central passage opens into chambers for human remains at this Neolithic burial mound.

Nunney Castle (Nunney, *Somerset*)

This 14th-century moated castle has a distinct French style. It was besieged in the Civil War and badly damaged.

Nympsfield Long Barrow (near Nympsfield, *Gloucestershire*)

This chambered Neolithic long barrow measures 27.5 metres (90 feet) in length.

O

Odda's Chapel (Deerhurst, *Gloucestershire*)

This rare Anglo-Saxon chapel is attached to a half-timbered farmhouse and probably dates from the 7th century.

Offa's Dyke (near Chepstow, *Gloucestershire*)

This is a 3-mile (5-kilometre) section of the large earthwork built by Offa, King of Mercia (757–796), which stretched from the Severn estuary to the Welsh coast and acted as a defensive boundary to his kingdom.

Offa's Dyke (*Powys*)

This was an earthen dyke that served as the first official boundary between England and Wales. It was ordered to be built by King Offa (AD 757–796), the ruler of the Midland Kingdom of Mercia. No one is sure why the dyke was constructed but there are many theories about the purpose it served, ranging from it being a defensive structure to an attempt to discourage cattle thieves. It is known that it was not designed to be permanently manned and that it was not a continuous structure. It covered a distance of 142 miles (227 kilometres), but there were many breaks along the wall, particularly where construction would have been difficult.

The dyke had a deep ditch on the Welsh side, which was overlooked by an earthwork barrier that was up to 6 metres (20 feet) high. Little remains today of this 1200-year-old structure but the best-preserved sections can be found in high, obscure places. There are some sections where the dyke stands almost to its full height. There is an Offa's Dyke Information Centre in Knighton, and this is a good place from which to explore the remains.

Ogmore Castle (Ogmore, *Bridgend*)

The 12th-century three-storey keep of this castle houses a hooded fireplace. A dry moat encircles the inner ward and the west wall stands 40 feet high.

Okehampton Castle (Okehampton, *Devon*)

These are the ruins of the largest castle in Devon, and they include the Norman motte and the remains of the keep.

Old Beaupre Castle (St Hilary, *Vale of Glamorgan*)

This ruined manor house was rebuilt during the 16th century and is noted for its Italianate gatehouse and porch.

Old Bishop's Palace *see* WOLVESEY CASTLE.

Old Blockhouse (Tresco, *Isles of Scilly*)

The remains of a small 16th-century gun tower can be seen at this site.

Old Bushmills Distillery (Bushmills, *County Antrim*)

Old Bushmills is the oldest licensed whisky distillery in the world. It was granted its licence in 1680.

Olderfleet Castle (Larne, *County Antrim*)

This 16th-century tower house is the last surviving of three that defended Larne.

Old Gorhambury House (near St Albans, *Hertfordshire*)

The remains of this Elizabethan mansion clearly indicate the impact that the Renaissance had on English architecture.

Old Manor, The (Norby, Ashbourne, *Derbyshire*)

This stone-built hall dates from the 13-15th centuries and has a rare kingpost roof, undercroft and cellars.

Old Owestry Hillfort (near Oswestry, *Shropshire*)

This impressive Iron Age fort is defended by a series of five ramparts and has an elaborate western entrance and unusual earthwork cisterns.

Old Royal Observatory (Docklands, London)

This was designed by Sir Christopher Wren in 1675.

Old Sarum (near Salisbury, *Wiltshire*)

This great earthwork was built by Iron Age people around 500 BC and was taken over by succeeding settlers and invaders. Old Sarum has been occupied by Romans, Saxons and Normans. It was one of the major strongholds of the Normans, and it had a royal castle and a grand cathedral. The settlement faded into insignificance as the city of Salisbury developed in the early 13th century. Today it is possible to see the remains of the fortress, the palace, castle and cathedral.

Old Slain's Castle (near Cruden Bay, *Aberdeenshire*)

The ruined tower remains from this fortress that belonged to Earl of Errol. It was destroyed in 1594 on the orders of James VI after he learned that the Earl was plotting to land Spanish troops on the Scottish coast.

Old Soar Manor (Plaxtol, *Kent*)

At this site it is possible to see the remains of a late 13th-century knight's manor house. The remains include a two-storey solar wing and a chapel.

Old Wardour Castle (near Tisbury, *Wiltshire*)

This 14th-century castle was destroyed in 1643 by a gunpowder explosion.

Orchardton Tower (near Castle Douglas, *Dumfries and Galloway*)

This charming small tower house, dating from the mid 15th century, is unique as it is circular in plan.

Orford Castle (Orford, *Suffolk*)

This royal castle was built in the 12th century to defend the coast. Of the remains, a splendid keep survives almost intact with three huge towers reaching to 27.5 metres (90 feet). Inside a spiral staircase leads to a maze of rooms and passages.

Ormiston Market Cross (Ormiston, *East Lothian*)

This 15th-century cross symbolizes the rights of the village's inhabitants to hold a market.

Oronsay Priory (Colonsay, *Argyll and Bute*)

The ruins of this 13th-century priory in the southern Inner Hebrides contain a 16th-century Celtic cross and high altar. The graveyard has stone slabs carved with portraits of warriors and saints.

Orphir, Earl's Bu and Church (near Kirkwall, *Orkney*)

The Earl's Bhu is the name for the foundations of ancient buildings that are thought to have been an Earl's palace in the Viking period. The church dates from the 12th century and consists of the chancel and part of the nave of the only medieval round church in Scotland.

Osborne House (near East Cowes, *Isle of Wight*)

This was where Queen Victoria and Prince Albert sought peace and quiet from the demands of court life. They bought the house in 1845 and immediately set about dismantling the original, relatively small house. The replacement house was designed by Thomas Cubitt and was Italianate in style. The main structure was finally completed in 1851. Albert died in 1861, and Victoria was never able to fully recover from the loss and she herself died here on 22 January 1901.

Otterburn (Otterburn, *Northumberland*)

In 1388 the Scots, under the Earl of Douglas, defeated the English and captured Sir Henry Percy (Harry Hotspur) here. Douglas was killed in the battle.

Oxford Castle (Oxford, *Oxfordshire*)

All that remains of this Norman castle built in 1071 are St George's Tower and the Mound.

Oxwich Castle (Oxwich, *Swansea*)

The remains of this 16th-century courtyard house built by the Mansel family can be seen here.

Oystermouth Castle (near Swansea, *Swansea*)

This impressive ruin on Mumbles Head was once the stronghold of the De Breose family. The remains include the gate-house, chapel and great hall, which date from the 13th or 14th centuries.

P

Paisley Abbey (Paisley, *Renfrewshire*)
The abbey was first founded in 1163, but much of the architecture that remains today dates from the 14th and 15th centuries, as do the stained glass windows and the organ, which is one of the finest in Europe.

Palace of Holyroodhouse (Edinburgh, *Edinburgh*)
The palace dates from the 15th century but was reconstructed in the 17th century for Charles II. After her return from France in 1561 Mary Queen of Scots spent six tragic years living here and it was the scene of the murder of David Rizzio. The palace is now the official Scottish royal residence.

Papcastle (Papcastle, *Cumbria*)
This is the site of a Roman fort.

Parc le Breos (Park Woods, near Penmaen, *Swansea*)
This prehistoric burial chamber is covered by a 21-metre (70-foot) long mound of stones. Also in Park Woods is Cathole Cave where the remains of prehistoric animals have been found.

Parliament House (Edinburgh, *Edinburgh*)
The seat of the Scottish government was built between 1632 and 1639 and was in use until the Union with England in 1707. Parliament House now houses the supreme law courts of Scotland.

Patterson's Spade Mill (Templepatrick, *County Antrim*)
This is the last surviving water-driven spade mill in Ireland.

Paxton's Tower (near Llandeilo, *Carmarthenshire*)

This triangular tower was built in 1811 by Sir William Paxton as a memorial to Lord Nelson.

Peel Castle (Peel, Isle of Man)

This vast fortress was built by the Lords of Man in the 15th century on the site of an old timber fort. The huge Round Tower that stands within the walls dates from the 10th century, and the ruins of St German's Cathedral date from the 13th century. The castle is on St Patrick's Isle and is linked to the mainland by a causeway.

Pembroke Castle (Pembroke, *Pembrokeshire*)

This 12th- to 13th-century fortress is noted for its impressive 24-metre (80-foot) high round keep. It is reputed to have been the birthplace of Henry VII in 1457. In 1648, it was partially destroyed during a siege by Parliamentarians.

Pen Caer (near Fishguard, *Pembrokeshire*)

This peninsula of volcanic rock is crowned by an Iron Age fort.

Pendennis Castle (Pendennis Head, *Cornwall*)

This is one half of the Cornish end of the chain of castles that Henry VIII built along the south coast of England in the period from 1539 to 1545 to defend it from French invasion. Pendennis Castle was adapted to protect England from French and Spanish invaders and continued to be used through to World War II.

Penhallam (near St Mary, *Cornwall*)

The ruins of this medieval manor house are surrounded by a defensive moat.

Penhow Castle (Penhow, *Newport*)

This is the oldest, inhabited castle in Wales. It was originally a small border fortress and was the first home of the famous British Seymour family.

Penmachno (Penmachno, *Conwy*)

The oldest Christian gravestones in Wales can be found here.
They date back to the 5th or 6th centuries.

Penmaenmawr (Penmaenmawr, *Conwy*)

A historical trail leads to the hill-top site of Stone Age flint
works.

Penmon (near Beaumaris, *Anglesey*)

The ruined monastery buildings at this site date from the 12th,
13th and 16th centuries.

Penrhos Cottage (Llanycefn, *Pembrokeshire*)

It was once local tradition that cottages built overnight on
common land could be claimed by the builders along with the
ground a stone's throw from the door. This thatched cottage is
an example of a cottage built in this tradition. It remained in
the family that built it until the 1960s.

Penrith Castle (Penrith, *Cumbria*)

This 14th-century red sandstone castle was built as a bastion
against raids from the north. The Beacon Hill tower was where
warning fires were lit during Border wars.

Pentre Ifan Burial Chamber (Newport, *Pembrokeshire*)

This was found to be part of a vanished long barrow when it
was excavated. The chamber remains include the capstone,
three uprights and a circular forecourt.

Pepperpot *see* ST CATHERINE'S ORATORY.

Pevensey Castle (Pevensey, *East Sussex*)

It was at Pevensey that William the Conquerer landed on 28
September 1066. It is thought that he and his troops may have
sheltered in the Roman shore fort of Anderida, within the
walls of which the Normans built a powerful stone fortress,
the ruins of which are still an impressive sight.

Peveril Castle (Castleton, *Derbyshire*)

The great square tower of this Norman castle stands almost to its original height. Sir Walter Scott used it as the setting for his novel *Peveril of the Peak*.

Picardy Symbol Stone (near Mireton, *Grampian*)

This 7th-century Pictish symbol stone is one of the oldest and simplest of its type.

Pickering Castle (Pickering, *North Yorkshire*)

This splendid motte-and-bailey castle was once a royal hunting lodge. The castle is well-preserved and retains much of the original walls, towers and keep.

Piel Castle (Piel Island, *Cumbria*)

The ruins of this 14th-century castle include the remains of the massive keep, inner and outer baileys, curtain walls and towers.

Piercebridge Roman Bridge (Piercebridge, *North Yorkshire*)

At this site are the remains of the stone piers and abutment of a Roman timber bridge that crossed the River Tees.

Pierowall Church (Westray, *Orkney*)

This medieval church, which is now just ruins, has tombstones with finely carved inscriptions.

Pike Hill Signal Tower (near Banks, *Cumbria*)

At this site it is possible to see the remains of a signal tower joined to HADRIAN'S WALL at a 45 degree angle.

Piper Sike Turret *see* LEAHILL TURRET.

Pitstone Windmill (Ivinghoe, *Buckinghamshire*)

This is one of the oldest post mills in Britain.

Planetrees Roman Wall (Low Brunton, *Northumberland*)

This 15-metre (50-foot) length of narrow wall standing on broad foundations indicates extensive rebuilding of HADRIAN'S WALL in Roman times.

Plas Mawr (Conwy, *Conwy*)

This is thought to be the best-preserved Elizabethan townhouse in Britain. it was built by Robert Wynn between 1576 and 1585. The gatehouse, stepped gables and lookout tower dominate the town.

Plas Newydd (near Bangor, *Anglesey*)

This magnificent 16th-century mansion was built for William Henry Paget, first Marquis of Anglesey, who was one of Wellington's trusted commanders.

Plas-yn-Rhiw (Plas-yn-Rhiw, *Gwynedd*)

This small manor house was begun in medieval times but has Tudor and Georgian additions.

Pluscarden Abbey (near Elgin, *Moray*)

This abbey, which was founded in 1230 by Alexander I, is still used for monastic services. The abbey was badly damaged in the 14th century and by 1560 it had fallen into ruin, but it was restored by Benedictine monks in 1948.

Poltross Burn Milecastle (near Gilsland, *Cumbria*)

This is one of the best-preserved milecastles of HADRIAN'S WALL. It has part of a flight of stairs leading to the top of the Wall, the remains of the gates and enclosing walls and barrack blocks.

Pontefract (Pontefract, *West Yorkshire*)

The castle here was founded in the 11th century, and part of the 13th- and 14th-century great tower remains, along with some walls.

Portchester Castle (Portchester, *Hampshire*)

The history of this castle stretches back over two thousand years. The Norman castle, built by Henry II, stands within the confines of the walls of a Roman fort. The remains of these Roman walls are among the most complete in Europe. It was at Portchester Castle that Henry V marshalled troops for the 1415 expedition to Agincourt.

Porth Hellick Down Burial Chamber (St Mary's, *Isles of Scilly*)

This burial mound, with its entrance passage and chamber, is considered to be the best-preserved Bronze Age burial mound on the island.

Porth Trecastell (near Aberffraw, *Anglesey*)

An ancient burial chamber with Stone Age wall carvings can be found on a headland at this site.

Portland Castle (Portland, *Dorset*)

This is one of the best preserved of the coastal forts built by Henry VIII. It is built of white Portland stone and was intended to repel the Spanish and the French. It changed hands many times during the Civil War.

Portsmouth Cathedral (Portsmouth, *Hampshire*)

Originally this was the Church of St Thomas of Canterbury, founded in 1185 and largely destroyed during the Civil War, but it was restored and made a cathedral in 1927.

Powis Castle (Welshpool, *Powys*)

This medieval castle was built in about 1200 for a Welsh prince. It has been inhabited continuously since its construction.

Prestatyn Castle (Prestatyn, *Denbighshire*)

The mound of a 12th-century castle stands in the town centre.

Preston Market Cross (near Prestonpans, *East Lothian*)

This is the only surviving example of a market cross of this type that remains on its original site. The cross is a beautiful example of early 17th-century design and has a cylindrical base surmounted by a cross-shaft headed by a unicorn.

Prestonpans (Prestonpans, *East Lothian*)

A cairn marks the site of the Battle of Prestonpans where the Jacobites saw victory during the 1745 uprising.

Princes Risborough Manor House (Princes Risborough, *Buckinghamshire*)

This 17th-century red-brick house has a fine Jacobean oak staircase.

Prior's Hall Barn (Widdington, *Essex*)

This is one of the best surviving medieval barns in southeast England. It is representative of the aisled barns of northwest Essex.

Prudhoe Castle (Prudhoe, *Northumberland*)

The extensive remains of this 12th-century castle include the gatehouse, curtain wall and keep.

Q

Quarley Hill (Quarley, *Hampshire*)

Situated here are the remains of an Iron Age hillfort that was abandoned before completion.

Quoyness Chambered Cairn (Sanday, *Orkney*)

This Neolithic cairn is a megalithic tomb that has triple retaining walls that contain a passage and a main chamber with six secondary cells.

R

Raglan Castle (near Raglan, *Monmouthshire*)

This impressive 15th-century castle was built by Sir William ap Thomas and his son William Herbert. The castle was attacked during the Civil War but much of the original building can still be seen today.

Ramsey Abbey Gatehouse (Ramsey, *Cambridgeshire*)

At this site it is possible to see the remains of a 15th-century gatehouse that belonged to the Benedictine abbey.

Ramsey Island (Ramsey Island, *Pembrokeshire*)

Legend tells that this holy island near St David's was formed by the 6th-century Breton saint Justinian, who cut it off from the mainland to ensure solitude.

Ranger's House (Blackheath, London)

This fine red-brick villa was built in 1700 on the edge of Greenwich Park. It has a splendid bow-windowed gallery.

Ratfyn Barrows (near Amesbury, *Wiltshire*)

This is part of a Bronze Age cemetery that contains burial mounds of different styles

Ravenglass Roman Bath House (near Ravenglass, *Cumbria*)

The walls of this bath-house are among the most complete Roman remains in Britain.

Ravenscraig Castle (near Kirkcaldy, *Fife*)

This is one of the earliest artillery forts in Scotland and was founded in 1460 by James II. It was later owned by the Sinclair Earls of Orkney. The fort consists of two round towers linked by a cross range. The west tower was the residence of Queen Mary of Guelders, the widow of James II.

Reculver Towers and Roman Fort (Reculver, *Kent*)

At this site there is a 12th-century landmark of twin towers and the remains of the walls of a Roman fort.

Restormel Castle (near Lostwithiel, *Cornwall*)

The large circular keep of this magnificent Norman castle remains in surprisingly good condition and is surrounded by a deep moat.

Rhuddlan Castle (Rhuddlan, *Denbighshire*)

Built in 1277, this was the second of Edward I's great Welsh fortifications. The castle is built to a concentric plan and is defended on one side by a protected river dock. It was burnt when the was besieged by Roundheads during the Civil War and has remained a ruin.

Rhug Chapel and Llangar Church (near Corwen, *Denbighshire*)

Rhug Chapel was built in 1637 and is noted for its glorious interior roof which is carried on the wings of wooden angels adorning the trusses. Nearby is the former parish church of All Saints Llangar with its important wall paintings dating from the 14th to the 18th centuries.

Richborough Castle Roman Fort (near Sandwich, *Kent*)

The fort and township at this site date back to the very first Roman landing in AD 43. Amongst the remains that survive today are the fortified walls and the foundations of a triumphal arch that stood 24 metres (80 feet) high.

Richborough Roman Amphitheatre (near Sandwich, *Kent*)

This is a ditch that is closely associated with the nearby 3rd-century castle.

Richmond Castle (Richmond, *North Yorkshire*)

This dramatic Norman fortress was built by William the Conqueror in his quest to quell the rebellious North. The site was chosen by William's ally, Alan of Brittany, as his principal castle and residence. The remains of the curtain wall and domestic buildings date from the 11th century, and the 30.5-metre (100-foot) high keep dates from the 12th century.

Legend tells that King Arthur lies in a local cave awaiting England's hour of need.

Ri Cruin Cairn (near Kilmartin, *Argyll and Bute*)

This Bronze Age cairn has had its covering removed to reveal three huge cists. One of the cist slabs has carvings of axe heads on one side.

Rievaulx Abbey (Rievaulx, *North Yorkshire*)

This Cistercian abbey was founded in 1131 and was home to a long line of Cistercian monks until the 16th century. The monks sought isolation from the outside world and held peace and solitude in high regard. Much of what the monks built has been destroyed or ruined, but most of the presbytery, the eastern part of the abbey church, stands to almost its original height. The abbey church was built in the 13th century to contain the shrine of St Aelred, the third abbot of the monastery.

Rievaulx Terrace and Temples (Rievaulx, *North Yorkshire*)
Two mid-18th-century temples and a $1/2$-metre (20-inch) long grass-covered terrace can be seen at this site.

Ring of Brogar Stone Circle and Henge (near Stromness, *Orkney*)
Of late Neolithic date, this is a splendid circle of upright stones with an enclosing ditch spanned by causeways.

Rispain Camp (near Whithorn, *Dumfries and Galloway*)
This rectangular settlement dating from the 1st or 2nd century AD is defended by a bank and a ditch.

Roche Abbey (near Maltby, *South Yorkshire*)
A Cistercian monastery was founded here in 1147 and excavation has revealed the full layout of the abbey.

Rochester Castle (Rochester Bridge, *Kent*)
This Norman bishop's castle was an important royal stronghold. It was built on the Roman city wall.

Roewen (Roewen, *Conwy*)
The Romans came here in the 1st century and drove roads across the hills and moors. To the west of the village a Roman road climbs to 427 metres (1400 feet) and crosses the mountains and moors which are scattered with standing stones and burial chambers.

Rollright Stones (near Chipping Norton, *Oxfordshire*)
These three groups of stones are known as The King's Men, The Whispering Knights and The King Stone. They span nearly two thousand years of the Neolithic and Bronze Ages.

Roman Bath (Strand Lane, London)
Restored in the 17th century, this may date from Roman times.

Roman Bath Inn (York, *North Yorkshire*)
This site has the remains of Roman steam baths and parts of the brick hot-air ducting.

Roman Baths (Bath, *Bath and North East Somerset*)

The Aquae Sulis spa resort is second only to HADRIAN'S WALL as a memorial to Roman Britain. The Latin name means 'waters of Sul', Sul was the name of a local Celtic god. The Roman buildings were about 6 metres (20 feet) below current street level. The main feature is the Great Bath, which is 21 metres (70 feet) long, 9 metres (30 feet) wide and 1.5 metres (5 feet) deep and is fed through Roman plumbing from the hot spring. The pool's original lead lining is intact. Nearby is the smaller King's Bath, which was the focal point of the Roman city and is believed to have been used by monarchs.

Roman Fort (Manchester)

Excavations have revealed that a fort was first built on this site in AD 79. The North Gate and part of the west wall of the Roman stronghold of Mancunium have been reconstructed.

Roman Wall (St Albans, *Hertfordshire*)

The Roman city of Verulamium was enclosed by a wall built in AD 200. The remains of towers, foundations of a gateway and a section of wall measuring several hundred metres can be seen today.

Roslin Chapel (Roslin, *Midlothian*)

This church was founded in 1446 by William St Clair, the third and last Prince of Orkney, and is noted for its lack of conformity with fashion or contemporary architecture. The church has a wealth of carvings, including the Apprentice Pillar. In the carvings there are references to the Knights of St Templar, Biblical stories, pagan symbols and the largest number of 'green men' that have ever be found in a medieval building. There are also carvings of plants from the New World, which are said to have been carved before Columbus discovered it.

Rotherwas Chapel (near Hereford, *Hereford and Worcester*)

This Roman Catholic chapel dates from the 14th and 16th cen-

turies. The mid-Victorian side chapel and high altar are notable features.

Rothesay Castle (Rothesay, Isle of Bute, *Argyll and Bute*)
This 13th-century castle of enclosure is circular in plan and
has a 16th-century forework. It was a favourite residence of
the Stewart kings.

Rough Castle (near Bonnybridge, Falkirk)
At this site it is possible to see the most complete earthworks
of a fort and the best-preserved length of rampart and ditch on
the ANTONINE WALL.

Rough Fort (Limavady, *County Londonderry*)
This is an early Christian rath.

Round Church (Cambridge, *Cambridgeshire*)
This circular Church of the Holy Sepulchre was built in 1130
by a crusading monastic order. It was built in imitation of the
original Holy Sepulchre in Jerusalem.

Royal Citadel (Plymouth, *Devon*)
This 17th-century fortress was built to defend the coastline
from Dutch invaders and is still in use today.

Royal Garrison Church (Portsmouth, *Hampshire*)
Although originally a hospice for pilgrims, this 16th-century
chapel was adapted as the garrison church following the dissolution of the monasteries. There is much of interest at this site,
but of particular note is the chancel.

Rudston (near Bridlington, *North Yorkshire*)
The tallest standing stone in Britain, 7.5 metres (25 feet) high,
can be found in the churchyard of All Saints. The size and
weight, 46 tonnes, of the stone are testament to the conviction
of the Neolithic people who erected it.

Rufford Abbey (near Ollerton, *Nottinghamshire*)
This 17th-century country house was built on the foundations
of a 12th-century Cistercian abbey.

ufus Stone (Minstead, *Hampshire*)

This marks the spot where William II (known as William Rufus because of his red complexion) was killed by an arrow whilst out hunting in 1100. It was erected in 1745.

Rushton Triangular Lodge (near Rushton, *Northamptonshire*)

This extraordinary building was built by the Catholic Sir Thomas Tresham after he was imprisoned for his religious beliefs. Completed in 1597, it symbolizes the Holy Trinity—it has three sides, three floors, trefoil windows and three triangular gables on each side.

Ruthven Barracks (near Kingussie, *Highland*)

Infantary barracks were erected at this site in 1719 following the 1715 Jacobite uprising. It has two ranges of quarters and a stable block. The barracks were captured and burned in 1746 by the army of Prince Charles Edward Stuart.

Ruthwell Cross (Ruthwell, *Dumfries and Galloway*)

Dating from the end of the 7th century AD, this Anglican cross, sculptured in high relief, is considered to be one of the major monuments of Europe in the Dark Ages.

Rycote Chapel (near Thame, *Oxfordshire*)

This 15th-century chapel has exquisitely carved and painted woodwork, two roofed pews and a musician's gallery.

S

Saddell Abbey (Saddell, *Argyll and Bute*)

This abbey was built in 1160 by Somerled, who liberated Argyll and Kintyre from Viking rule. The remains include carved tombstones from the early 14th to the late 16th centuries, which depict armoured warriors and priests. Somerled, who was king of Man and the Isles, is believed to be buried here.

St Albans (St Albans, *Hertfordshire*)

This was where the Romans built the city of Verulamium by the River Ver. Walls, amphitheatre and mosaic floors all remain well preserved. The cathedral stands on the hill where the Christian martyr St Alban was beheaded.

St Andrews Castle (St Andrews, *Fife*)

Today it is possible to see the ruins of castle of the archbishops of St Andrews, which dates in part from the 13th century. The 'bottle' dungeon is a notable feature, as are the mine and counter-mine that were tunnelled during the seige after Cardinal Beaton was murderd in 1546.

St Andrews Cathedral and St Rule's Tower (St Andrews, *Fife*)

The remains of the largest cathedral in Scotland, which were founded in 1160, are today only a ruined fragment of what was once an impressive piece of architecture. St Rule's Tower, dating from the early 12th century, is part of the first church of the Augustinian canons at St Andrews.

St Andrews (Penrith, *Cumbria*)

Owen Caesarius, 10th-century Cumbrian ruler, is said to be buried in the churchyard here in the ancient Giant's Grave. The Church of St Andrew was rebuilt in the 18th century but has a Norman west tower.

St Asaph (near Bodelwyddan, *Denbighshire*)

This is Britain's smallest cathedral. It was founded in AD 560 by St Kentigern and was rebuilt in the late 15th century and restored in the 19th century.

St Augustine's Abbey (Canterbury, *Kent*)

This is part of the World Heritage Site complex at CANTERBURY and is of significant historical importance. St Augustine's Abbey is considered to be the 'cradle of Christianity' in England and was founded by St Augustine 1400 years ago. He built the great shrine one year after arriving in England, and it became the centre of the English Christian movement. St Augustine is buried at the abbey, as are the early Archbishops of Canterbury.

Although many of the abbey buildings were destroyed by Henry VIII during the dissolution of the monasteries, it is still possible to see the remains of the foundations of the original 6th-century church. Fragments of the St Pancras chapel, made from Roman brick, and sections of the Norman church and medieval monastery also survive.

St Augustine's Cross (Ebbsfleet, *Kent*)

This 19th-century Celtic style cross marks the site where St Augustine landed in 597.

St Barr, Church of *see* CILLE BHARRA.

St Benet's Abbey (near Norwich, *Norfolk*)

The ruins of this Benedictine monastery surround a Georgian windmill. The gatehouse is largely intact, as are the outer walls and church foundations.

St Botolph's Priory (Colchester, *Essex*)

This was the first Augustinian priory in England. The remains of the nave, with an impressive arcaded west end, can still be seen today.

St Breock Downs Monolith (St Breock Downs, *Cornwall*)

This prehistoric standing stone was once nearly five metres (16 feet) high.

St Bridget's Kirk (Dalgety, *Fife*)

At this site is the shell of a medieval church that was greatly altered in the 17th century for Protestant worship. In the west end there is a burial vault with a laird's loft above it that was built for the Earl of Dunfermline.

St Cadfan's Church (Tywyn, *Gwynedd*)

At this church there is a 2-metre (7-foot) high stone bearing what is thought to be 7th-century Welsh inscriptions.

St Cassian's Church (Chaddesley Corbett, near Kidderminster, *Hereford and Worcester*)

This mainly 14th-century church has a Norman nave and a 12th-century font dedicated to a martyred teacher who was murdered by pagan pupils.

St Catherine's Castle (Fowey, *Cornwall*)

This small fort was built by Henry VIII to protect Fowey harbour.

St Catherine's Oratory (near Niton, *Isle of Wight*)

This 14th-century lighthouse was constructed after the wine ship *St Marie* was wrecked. It stands on the island's highest point and is affectionately known as the Pepperpot.

St Cwyfan's Church (near Aberffraw, *Anglesey*)

This small church was built 1300 years ago and was restored in 1893.

St Cybi's Well (Llangybi, *Gwynedd*)

This well is famous for its curative properties. St Cybi was a 6th-century Cornish saint who healed the sick.

St David's Bishop's Palace (St David's, *Pembrokeshire*)

This imposing palace stands within the perimeter of the cathedral precincts. The surviving buildings mostly date from the 14th century. The arcaded parapet by Bishop Henry de Gower is of particular note.

St David's Cathedral (St David's, *Pembrokeshire*)

St David is said to have founded a monastic settlement on this site in the 6th century. In 1181 the cathedral was built and was altered in the 12th, 14th and 16th centuries. These alterations give it a variety of architectural styles.

St Dunstan and All Saints Church (Docklands, London)

The Saxon stone rood is all that remains of the earliest church in Stepney. It was rebuilt in the 10th century by St Dunstan and was altered in the 15th and 19th centuries.

St Florence (St Florence, *Pembrokeshire*)

Norman kings encouraged people from Flanders to settle here during the 12th century.

St George's Chapel (Windsor, *Berkshire*)

This is the finest example of Perpendicular architecture in England. It was founded in 1477 by Edward IV for the Knights of the Garter and as a burial place for royalty.

St George's Guildhall (King's Lynn, *Norfolk*)

This is the largest surviving English guildhall, and it has an adjoining medieval warehouse.

St Giles' Cathedral (City of Edinburgh)

The High Kirk of Edinburgh dates from the 15th century and is noted for its Crown spire. Also of note is the tiny Thistle Chapel, built in dedication to the Order of the Thistle, the highest order of chivalry in Scotland, which features two carved angels playing bagpipes.

St Giles' Church *see* SKELTON.

St James's Chapel (Lindsey, *Suffolk*)

This is a small 13th-century chapel that has a thatched roof and lancet windows.

St James's Palace (Westminster, London)

This was built in the 16th century by Henry VIII. The Chapel Royal was built in 1532 and has a painted ceiling commemorating the marriage of Henry VIII and Anne of Cleves.

St John's Abbey Gate (Colchester, *Essex*)

This fine abbey gatehouse survives from the Benedictine abbey of St John.

St John's Church (Cardiff, *Cardiff*)

This parish church dates from 1453 and has a 40-metre (130-foot) tower that was added in 1473. In the Herbert Chapel there is a monument to two brothers (Sir William Herbert, Keeper of Cardiff Castle, who died in 1609 and Sir John

Herbert, private secretary to Elizabeth I, who died in 1617).

St John's Commandery (Swingfield Minnis, *Kent*)

This medieval chapel has a fine moulded plaster ceiling and an impressive timber roof. It was converted into a farmhouse during the 16th century.

St John's Gate (Bristol, *Bristol*)

This is the city's last medieval gate, and the mythical kings, Brennus and Belinus, who are said to have founded Bristol, look down from above it.

St John the Baptist, Church of (Chester, *Cheshire*)

This was originally founded by the Saxon princess Aethelflaeda and was for a time the cathedral of Mercia. It is an impressive sight with the Norman pillars of the nave rising to a Transitional triforium and early clerestory. The ruins of the collapsed northwest tower stand outside.

St Leonard's Tower (West Malling, *Kent*)

This early Norman tower was built by Gundulph, Bishop of Rochester, in 1080.

St Levan (near Porthcurno, *Cornwall*)

This medieval church, dedicated to St Levan, who is said to have landed on a nearby beach in the 6th or 7th century, contains carved pews. The Celtic cross that stands outside is older than the church itself.

St Lythans (St Lythans, near Cardiff, *Cardiff*)

Dating from 2500 BC, this Neolithic burial chamber has strong stone pillars and capstone. Nearby, of similar date, is Tinkinswood Tomb, which has a 40-tonne capstone. The bones of 50 people were found in this burial chamber.

St Magnus Cathedral (Kirkwall, *Orkney*)

With Glasgow Cathedral, this red sandstone building was one of only two medieval cathedrals to survive the Reformation intact. It was founded in 1138 in memory of Magnus, Earl of

Orkney, who was murdered in 1115 on the island of Egilsay.

St Magnus, Church of (Egilsay, *Orkney*)

This 12th-century church is roofless but otherwise intact. The round tower and impressive location can be admired today.

St Mary, Chapel of *see* CILLE BHARRA.

St Mary's Church (Kempley, *Gloucestershire*)

This Norman church has splendid wall paintings dating from the 12th to 14th centuries.

St Mary's Church (Studley Royal, *North Yorkshire*)

This splendid Victorian church was designed by William Burges in the 1870s and has a highly decorated interior. Remaining in their original glory are gilted and painted figures, a splendid organ, coloured marble and stained glass.

St Mary's Church (Wedmore, *Somerset*)

The Treaty of Wedmore was signed here in AD 878 by King Alfred following his defeat of the Danes at the Battle of Ethendune.

St Mary and St Sexburga, Church of (Minster, *Kent*)

Founded in AD 674, this is one of the oldest places of Christian worship in England. The cruciform church has a Norman nave.

St Mary's Church, Kirkheugh (St Andrews, *Fife*)

The scanty foundations of a small cruciform church are the remains of what was the earliest collegiate church in Scotland. It was destroyed during the Reformation.

St Mary's Kirk (near Lumsden, *Aberdeenshire*)

This, although roofless, is one of the finest medieval parish churches in Scotland and is still largely intact. The early Romanesque doorway and early 16th-century sacrament house are both of note.

St Mary's Priory *see* DEVENISH ISLAND.

St Mawes Castle (St Mawes, *Cornwall*)

This, along with PENDENNIS, was built by Henry VIII to defend the entrance to safe anchorage in Carrick Roads. It has three circular bastions with gun ports and is a formidable sight.

St Michael's Mount (Marazion, *Cornwall*)

The spectacular castle that sits on this famous rocky island dates from the 14th century and is built on the site of what was originally a Benedictine chapel. At the castle it is possible to see early rooms, a rococo Gothic drawing room and a 14th-century church.

St Michael, Church of (Oxford, *Oxfordshire*)

The 11th-century tower is the oldest building in Oxford. The east window, dating from 1290, is the oldest example of stained glass in Oxford.

St Molaise's house *see* Devenish Island.

St Ninian's Cave (near Whithorn, *Dumfries and Galloway*)

The crosses of various dates carved on the walls of the cave are now weathered, but early crosses that were found here are now at Whithorn museum.

St Olave's Priory (near Great Yarmouth, *Norfolk*)

This Augustinian priory was named after the patron saint of Norway and was founded nearly two hundred years after his death in 1030.

St Orland's Stone (near Forfar, *Angus*)

This early Christian sculptured slab has a cross on one side and Pictish figures and symbols on the other.

St Paul's Cathedral (City of London, *London*)

This cathedral was built by Christopher Wren following the destruction of the previous cathedral in the Great Fire of 1666.

St Paul's Monastery and Bede's World Museum (Jarrow, Tyne and Wear)

This was the home of the Venerable Bede and survives partly as the chancel of the parish church. St Paul's monastery is one of the best-understood Anglo-Saxon monastic sites.

St Peter's Church (Barton-on-Humber, North *Lincolnshire*)
This 15th-century former parish church has an Anglo-Saxon tower and baptistry.

St Rule's Tower *see* ST ANDREWS CATHEDRAL.

St Trinuana's Chapel, Restalrig Collegiate Church (Edinburgh)
At this site there is the lower part of a chapel built by James III, housing the shrine of St Trinuana who was a Pictish saint. The chapel has a unique vaulted chamber that is hexagonal in shape.

St Vigeans Sculptured Stones (near Arbroath, *Angus*)
This fine collection of over thirty early Christian and Pictish stones is housed in cottages in the village of St Vigeans.

Salcombe (Salcombe, *Devon*)
A plaque commemorating the Americans who sailed from this town to the World War II D-Day landings can be seen in Normandy Way.

Salisbury Cathedral (Salisbury, *Wiltshire*)
This cathedral was founded in 1220 and largely completed by 1260. The spire was not added until one hundred years later, and at 123 metres (404 feet) it is the tallest spire in England. The cathedral also houses a 1386 clock, and it is claimed that this is the oldest clock in the world. The vaulted colonnades of the cloisters and the octagonal chapterhouse are also of interest. The library treasures include an original copy of the Magna Carta.

Salisbury Plain (Salisbury Plain, *Wiltshire*)
Although largely deserted today, this was once the site of many communities. Settlers from the Stone Age, Bronze Age and Iron Age have left hundreds of burial mounds scattered over the chalklands.

Sanctuary, The (near West Kennet, *Wiltshire*)
The Sanctuary, thought to be about 5000 years old, consists of

two concentric stone circles and six timber uprights indicated by concrete pots.

Sandbach Crosses (Sandbach, *Cheshire*)

These rare Saxon crosses date from the 9th century and are carved with animals, dragons and biblical scenes.

Sanquhar (Sanquhar, *Dumfries and Galloway*)

This town is home to Britain's oldest Post Office, which was first opened in 1763 and operates to this day. The town also has a monument that pays tribute to two declarations made by the Covenanters renouncing their allegiance first to Charles II in 1680 and then to James VII in 1685.

Sawley Abbey (Sawley, *Lancashire*)

This Cistercian abbey was founded in 1147.

Scarborough Castle (Scarborough, *North Yorkshire*)

The buttressed castle walls of this huge 12th-century castle stretch out along the cliff edge, and the remains of the rectangular stone keep stand over three storeys high. The castle was blasted by cannons during the Civil War and bombarded during World War I but still remains a spectacular site. There is also the site of a 4th-century Roman signal station.

Scone Palace (Perth, *Perth and Kinross*)

This is one of Scotland's grandest stately homes. It was once the traditional crowning place of Scottish monarchs. The original buildings date from the 16th century, but much of what can be seen today dates from the its enlargement in 1803.

Scott Monument (Edinburgh)

This marble statue of the novelist Sir Walter Scott was designed by George Meikle Kemp and was completed in 1844. It stands 61 metres (200 feet) high and is a confection of neo-Gothic spires, crockets, gargoyles and niches. The monument has many statues of characters from Scott's novels, including Rob Roy, Ivanhoe and John Knox.

Segontium Roman Fort (Caernarfon, *Gwynedd*)

This was once the site of a Roman fort. The museum tells the story of the Roman conquest and occupation of Wales.

Selby Abbey (Selby, *North Yorkshire*)

This three-towered limestone Norman abbey dates from 1069, but after being badly damaged by fire it was restored in 1906.

Semer Water (near Bainbridge, *North Yorkshire*)

Legend tells that there is a lost city lying at the bottom of this lake left over from the Ice Age. On the shores of the lake Celtic and Roman remains have been found.

Seton Collegiate Church (near Cockenzie, *East Lothian*)

This lovely building has a chancel and apse dating from the 15th century and transepts and steeple that were built by the widow of the Lord Seton who was killed in 1513 at the Battle of Flodden.

Sewingshields Hall (near Bardon Mill, *Northumberland*)

At this site near HOUSESTEADS FORT there are the remains of the Sewingshields milecastle and turret and Grindon and Coesike turrets of HADRIAN'S WALL.

Shane's Castle (Antrim, *County Antrim*)

The first castle on this site was built in the 17th century. The castle was redisgned by Nash in the 19th century but was destroyed by fire before the work was completed. A second castle was built in the mid-19th century but this too was gutted by fire during the troubles of 1922.

Shap Abbey (near Shap, *Cumbria*)

Remains of this Premonsratensian abbey include the tower, which is an impressive sight.

Sherborne Old Castle (near Sherborne, *Dorset*)

It took Cromwell sixteen days to capture this 12th-century castle during the Civil War. It was later abandoned and is now in ruins.

Sherburn in Elmet (Sherburn in Elmet, *North Yorkshire*)

The late Norman church that can be seen here is built on the site of an earlier Saxon church dating from the old kingdom of Elmet days.

Sheriff Hutton (Sheriff Hutton, *North Yorkshire*)

The 14th-century castle that dominates the village was once the seat of Richard III.

Shute Barton (Shute, *Devon*)

This is one of the most important surviving non-fortified manor houses of the Middle Ages. Building commenced in 1380, and it was finally completed in the late 16th century. It was partly demolished towards the end of the 18th century. Of note are the battlemented turrets, late Gothic windows and the Tudor gatehouse.

Sidney Sussex College (Cambridge, *Cambridgeshire*)

This was founded in 1594, and one of its most famous students was Oliver Cromwell. His embalmed head is believed to be buried in a secret place in the antechapel.

Silbury Hill (near West Kennet, *Wiltshire*)

This artificial prehistoric mound is the largest Neolithic construction of its type in Europe.

Silchester Roman City Walls and Amphitheatre (near Silchester, *Hampshire*)

These Roman town walls are the best-preserved in Britain. They measure almost 1½ miles (2.4 kilometres) around, and there is also an impressive amphitheatre that has recently been restored.

Sir Bevil Grenville's Monument (Lansdown, *Bath and North East Somerset*)

This monument commemorates the heroism of this Royalist commander and his Cornish pikemen at the Battle of Lansdown in 1643. Sir Bevil was killed in the battle.

Sizergh Castle (Sizergh, *Cumbria*)

This 14th-century peel tower was extended in Tudor times and houses some of the finest examples of Elizabethan carved overmantels in Britain. This has been the family home of the Strickland family for over 750 years.

Skara Brae Prehistoric Village (near Kirkwall, *Orkney*)

This is the best-preserved group of Stone Age houses in western Europe. It lay buried beneath sand until a storm revealed it in 1850. At this prehistoric site it is possible to see 5000-year-old stone dressers, beds and cupboards.

Skelton (Skelton, *North Yorkshire*)

The church of St Giles that can be seen here dates from 1250. It is well preserved and is unusual in that it has later additions.

Skenfrith Castle (Skenfrith, *Monmouthshire*)

This 13th-century castle was one of the three 'trilateral' castles built by Hubert de Burgh to defend the Welsh Marches, the others being GROSMONT CASTLE and WHITE CASTLE. It has a round keep that is set within a towered curtain wall.

Sketrick Castle (Killinchy, *County Down*)

This tall tower house is thought to date from the 15th century. Although it was badly ruined, there are remains that include a boat bay and prison.

Skipsea Castle (near Bridlington, *East Riding of Yorkshire*)

The earthworks at this site are the remains of a Norman motte-and-bailey castle.

Slains Castle *see* OLD SLAINS CASTLE.

Slapton Ley (near Slapton, *Devon*)

A monument commemorating the 639 US soldiers killed by German U-boats that ran into a Normandy landing rehearsal can be seen here.

Slash Hollow (Snipe Dales, *Lincolnshire*)

This was the site of the 1643 Civil War Battle of Winceby.

Smailholm Tower (near Smailholm, *Scottish Borders*)

This small rectangular tower is set within a barmkin wall (a stout defensive wall) on a rocky outcrop and is five storeys high with 2-metre (7-foot) thick walls.

Souter Lighthouse (Whitburn, *Tyne and Wear*)

This shore-based lighthouse was the first to operate using alternating eletric current. It was opened in 1871.

South Foreland Lighthouse (St Margaret's at Cliffe, *Kent*)

This distinctive landmark on the White Cliffs of Dover was built in 1843 and was used by Marconi for the first radio communications in 1843.

Southampton (Southhampton, *Hampshire*)

Southampton has been an important site in many an historic event. It was from here that the Pilgrim Fathers set sail in the *Mayflower* in 1620. The *Titanic* also set sail from here. It was at Southampton that King Canute is said to have tried to turn back the tide.

Southsea Castle (Portsmouth, *Hampshire*)

This was built in 1545 by Henry VIII as part of the chain of coastal forts for protecting the southern coast of England.

Springhill (Moneymore, *County Londonderry*)

This manor house dates back to the 17th century and was originally the home of the Scottish Conyngham family.

Spynie Palace (near Elgin, *Moray*)

This was the residence of the Moray bishops from the 14th century to 1686. The site is dominated by a tower built by Bishop David Stewart.

Stamford Bridge (Stamford Bridge, *North Yorkshire*)

Harold of England defeated Harold of Norway here in a battle in 1066.

Staneydale 'Temple' (near Walls, *Shetland*)

This Neolithic hall is heel-shaped externally and contains a large, oval chamber. Surrounding it are ruins of houses, cairns and walls dating from the same period in history.

Stanton Drew Circles and Cove (Stanton Drew, *Bath and North East Somerset*)

This is one of the finest Neolithic religious sites in Britain. It has three stone circles, two stone avenues and a burial chamber.

Stanwick Iron Age Fortifications (Forcett, *North Yorkshire*)

This was the tribal stronghold of the Brigantes tribe. The vast earthworks covered 850 acres. Today it is possible to see an excavated section of ditch cut into the rock and the rampart.

Staunton Harold Church (Staunton Harold, *Leicestershire*)

This is one of the very few churches to be constructed during the Commonwealth of Oliver Cromwell. It was erected by Sir Robert Shirley, an ardent Royalist. The interior retains its original 17th-century cushions and hangings and also includes painted ceilings and fine panelling. There is a wrought-iron screen that was designed by Robert Bakewell.

Steeton Hall Gateway (near Castleford, *North Yorkshire*)

This a good example of a well-preserved 14th-century gatehouse.

Stembridge Tower Mill (High Ham, *Somerset*)

This is the last thatched windmill in England. It dates from 1822 and was in use until 1910.

Stirling Castle (Stirling, *Stirling*)

This is the grandest of all the castles in Scotland with its commanding positioning on a rocky outcrop. By 1124, when Alexander I died here, it was several centuries old and had become an important royal residence and at various times was the country's capital. It was held several times by the English, being retaken in 1297 by William Wallace before being besieged and captured by Edward I in 1304. It was taken by Cromwell's army under General Monk in 1651 and was unsuccessfully besieged by Prince Charlie in 1646. The castle has many interesting features (the Great Hall and Gatehouse of James IV, the Palace of James V, the Chapel Royal, which was modelled by James VI, and artillery fortifications of the 16th and 18th centuries).

Stirling Old Bridge (Stirling, *Stirling*)

This bridge was built in the late 15th century, but the four southernmost arches were rebuilt in 1749 after the bridge was blown up during the 1745 uprisings to prevent the Stuart army entering Stirling.

Stoke Gabriel (Stoke Gabriel, *Devon*)

This village has a medieval church with a Norman tower, and the churchyard has an enormous yew tree thought to be about a thousand years old.

Stokesay Castle (near Ludlow, *Shropshire*)

This is the finest medieval manor house in England. The castle now stands in a group with its own splendid timber-framed Jacobean gatehouse and the parish church.

Stoke-sub-Hamdon Priory (Stoke-sub-Hamdon, *Somerset*)

This complex of buildings was built in the 14th century for the priests of the chantry chapel of St Nicholas, which no longer exists.

Stonegate (York, *North Yorkshire*)

This is one of the city's best-preserved medieval streets. It follows the path of an earlier Roman road.

Stonehenge (near Amesbury, *Wiltshire*)

The great and ancient stone circle here is one of Britain's most famous historic sites and is considered to be one of the wonders of the world. The massive stones that remain today are only part of the original prehistoric complex. Some of the ceremonial and domestic structures that have been found in the surrounding landscape are thought to be older than the monument itself. The construction of Stonhenge is thought to have taken place in various stages between 3000 BC and 1600 BC. In about 3000 BC, the outer circular bank and ditch were constructed and the massive Heel Stone was placed at the entrance to the central enclosure. Just inside the ditch, a ring of 56 pits was dug, now known as Aubrey Holes. These pits were later filled with human ashes and dirt. Around 2100 BC, the first stone circle was raised within the earthworks, consisting of 80 great blocks of bluestone, weighing up to 40 tonnes each, cut from quarries in Wales and somehow transported to this site. In 1500 BC, the incomplete bluestone circle was transformed by the construction of 25 trilithons (two upright stones crossed by a lintel) and an inner horseshoe formation of 5 trilithons. Made from Marlborough Downs sandstone, these huge stones were masterfully dressed and worked. A further small circle and horseshoe were erected within the trilithons.

No one is entirely sure what purpose Stonehenge served. It is known that it served as a focal point for thousands of years within a ceremonial landscape. The most popular theory is that it was a time-measuring device or an observatory of some sort. This theory is supported by the fact that the structures were all built in alignment towards the points of sunrise and sunset on the summer and winter soltices and that the site is symmetrical and located on a slight rise in a flat valley.

Stonehenge is testament to the ingenuity and resourcefulness of its builders. They managed to create this amazing monument with the most basic of tools. The society that was able to command the amount of labour to design and construct this structure must have been very sophisticated indeed. It is not known how the builders managed to transport the huge stones that they used to create this monument, but it is certain that it required huge effort to move, shape and raise them.

At this site it is also possible to see evidence of burial

mounds that are thought to contain the graves of ruling families, the long barrows of the New Stone Age and the various types of barrows that followed. There are also visible remains of earthworks and monuments, including the long, oval earthwork to the north, the Cursus.

Stone of Sorrow see CLACH A'CHARRIDH.

Stoney Littleton Long Barrow (near Wellow, *Bath and North East Somerset*)

This Neolithic burial mound measures 30 metres (100 feet) long and has chambers where human remains once lay.

Strangford Castle (Strangford, *County Down*)

This three-storey tower house was built in the 16th century.

Strata Florida Abbey (near Pontrhydfendigaid, *Ceredigion*)

This now ruined abbey was once magnificent. It was founded in 1197 by Rhys ap Gruffudd but was virtually destroyed in the uprising led by Owain Glyndwr. The remains include two pointed archways set in the remains of the north and east walls of the church's central tower.

Struell Wells (Downpatrick, *County Down*)

Pilgrims once came to collect healing water from these holy drinking and eye wells. The ruins of an 18th-century church and single-sex bath houses lie nearby.

Studley Royal Water Garden see FOUNTAINS ABBEY.

Sudeley Castle (near Cheltenham, *Gloucestershire*)

This medieval fortress has a ruined banqueting hall and the tomb of Catherine Parr, the sixth wife of Henry VIII.

Sueno's Stone (Forres, *Aberdeenshire*)

This is the most remarkable sculptured monument in Britain and is probably a cenotaph. It is over 6 metres (20 feet) high and dates from the end of the first millenium AD.

Sutton House (Hackney, London)

This is a rare example of a Tudor red-brick house, which was built in 1535 by Sir Rafe Sadleir, principal secretary of state for Henry VIII. Of particular note are the original linefold panelling and the 17th-century wall paintings.

Sutton Scarsdale Hall (near Chesterfield, *Derbyshire*)

This is the dramatic hilltop shell of an early 18th-century baroque mansion.

Sutton Valence Castle (near Maidstone, *Kent*)

This 12th-century stone keep was built to watch over the important medieval route across the Weald from Rye to Maidstone. Today, just ruins remain.

Swanage Bay (Swanage, *Dorset*)

King Alfred beat the Danes in a battle here in 877.

Sweetheart Abbey (New Abbey, *Dumfries and Galloway*)

This is a splendid ruin of a late 13th-century abbey founded by Dervogilla, Lady of Galloway (who is buried here), in memory of her husband, John Balliol. Thirty acres are enclosed by a well-preserved precinct wall.

T

Taddington Moor Chambered Cairn (near Buxton, *Derbyshire*)

A huge barrow was built here 4500 years ago. Two limestone burial chambers remain.

Talley Abbey (Talley, *Carmarthenshire*)

This Cistercian abbey was founded in 1131. Its remarkably complete abbey church was rebuilt in the late 13th century.

Tamworth (Tamworth, *Staffordshire*)

This was the historic Saxon capital of Mercia. The fine Norman motte-and-bailey castle spans centuries. The keep, tower and herring-bone curtain wall date from 1180s while other parts are from later periods.

Tantallon Castle (near North Berwick, *East Lothian*)

This remarkable fortification is built on a promontory looking out to the Bass Rock and has earthwork defences and a massive 14th-century curtain wall with towers. The castle was further strengthened during the 16th century.

Tattershall Castle (Tattershall, *Lincolnshire*)

This huge fortified tower was built in the mid-15th century for Ralph Cromwell, Lord Treasurer of England. It is an important example of an early brick building and has a tower containing state apartments.

Tattershall College (Tattershall, *Lincolnshire*)

This grammar school for church choristers was built in the mid 15th century by Ralph, Lord Cromwell, who also built the nearby TATTERSHALL CASTLE.

Tatton Park (Knutsford, *Cheshire*)

This is one of the most complete historic estates in England that is open to visitors. The 19th-century Wyatt house contains the Egerton family's collection of pictures, books, china, glass, silver and furniture. Also of note are the servants' quarters, cellars, medieval old hall and 18th-century farm.

Taversoe Tuick Chambered Cairn (Rousay, *Orkney*)

This megalithic chambered mound has two burial chambers, one above the other, and is of Neolithic date.

Teampull Mor *see* DEVENISH ISLAND.

Temple Church (Bristol, *Bristol*)

The tower and walls of this 15th-century church escaped destruction from the bombs of World War II.

Temple Manor (Rochester, *Kent*)

This was the 13th-century manor house of the Knights Templar.

Temple of Mithras (near Chollerton, *Northumberland*)

The remains of this 3rd-century temple and facsimiles of altars were found here during excavations.

Temple of the Winds *see* MOUNT STEWART HOUSE AND TEMPLE OF THE WINDS.

Templetown Mausoleum (Templepatrick, *County Antrim*)
This family mausoleum was designed by Robert Adam and is situated in the grounds of Castle Upton.

Temple Wood Stone Circles (near Kilmartin, *Argyll and Bute*)
At this site, near NETHER LARGIE, there is a circle of upright stones as well as the remains of an earlier circle dating from about 3000 BC.

Tenby Tudor Merchant's House (Tenby, *Pembrokeshire*)
This is a fine example of gabled 15th-century architecture. Three of the walls show the remains of frescoes.

Tewkesbury (Tewkesbury, *Gloucestershire*)
This ancient town is where the Lancastarians were defeated by the Yorkists in 1471 during the War of the Roses.

Theatre Royal (Bury St Edmunds, *Suffolk*)
This rare example of a late Georgian playhouse was built by William Wilkins in 1819.

Thetford Priory (Thetford, *Norfolk*)
The remains of this Cluniac priory, founded in 1103, include a 14th-century gatehouse and the plan of the cloisters.

Thetford Warren Lodge (near Thetford, *Norfolk*)
This small, two-storey medieval house was probably the home of the gamekeeper of Thetford Priory. Ruins are all that remain of this house today.

Thorington Hall (Stoke-by-Nayland, *Essex*)
This oak-framed, plastered, gabled house was originally built in about 1600 and was extended around 1700.

Thorney (Thorney, *Lincolnshire*)
The Saxon rebel Hereward the Wake made his last stand against the invading Norman troops here. The Saxon abbey was rebuilt by the Normans in 1085.

Thornton Abbey and Gatehouse (near Scunthorpe, North Lincolnshire)

This ruined 12th-century Augustinian priory has a splendid brick gatehouse.

Threave Castle (near Castle Douglas, *Dumfries and Galloway*)

This massive tower was built in the late 14th century by Archibald the Grim, Lord of Galloway. The castle, which stands on an island in the River Dee, was attacked in 1455 by James II.

Tilbury Fort (near Tilbury, *Essex*)

This is the largest and best-preserved example of 17th-century military engineering in England. It has a commanding position overlooking the Thames, and its fortifications have been developed over a 200-year period.

Tinkinswood Tomb *see* ST LYTHANS.

Tintagel Castle (Tintagel, *Cornwall*)

The black, gaunt ruins of Tintagel Castle boast a spectacular location on one of England's most dramatic coastlines at Tintagel Head. Legend tells that this was the birthplace of King Arthur, a notion first made popular by the 12th-century chronicler, Geoffrey of Monmouth. The castle ruins in fact belong to a Norman stronghold built in 1145 for the Earl of Cromwell. The castle was eventually allowed to fall into decay, and much of it had been washed into the sea by the 16th century.

Tintagel was a Roman settlement and military outpost and then the stronghold of a Celtic king during the 5th and 6th centuries. There is an early Christian church on the site of what some think may have been a cemetery for important men. It is thought that one of these important men may have been King Mark, whose nephew Tristan fell in love with Iseult (Isolde). This couple's doomed romance is part of Tintagel's story, as are Geoffrey of Monmouth's tales, in which Uther Pendragon, aided by Merlin, seduced Queen Igerna at Tintagel.

Tintagel Old Post Office (Tintagel, *Cornwall*)

This small and interesting 14th-century stone house was built to the plan of a medieval manor house. In the 19th century it was used as a letter-receiving office for the district. It was used for this purpose for fifty years and has now been restored to that function.

Tintern Abbey (Tintern Parva, *Monmouthshire*)

The ruins of this Cistercian monastery church are still relatively intact. The monastery was founded in 1131 and was prosperous well into the 15th century. The monastery was closed during the dissolution of the monasteries, and most of the buildings, other than the church, were destroyed.

Titchfield Abbey (near Titchfield, *Hampshire*)

The remains of this 13th-century abbey are overlooked by a grand Tudor gatehouse.

Tolbooth Steeple (City of Glasgow)

This steeple is seven storeys and 38 metres (126 feet) high and is the sole remnant of the tolbooth that stood on this site in 1626.

Tolquhon Castle (near Pitmedden, *Aberdeenshire*)

This castle was built for the Forbes family and has a 15th-century tower that was enlarged by William Forbes between 1584 and 1589. It is noted for its highly ornamented gatehouse.

Tomen-y-Mur (near Trawsfynydd, *Gwynedd*)

The remains of an amphithehatre, bath buildings, parade ground and burial mounds can all be seen at the site of this 1st- or 2nd-century Roman fort. Within the outline of the fort stands the motte of an early medieval castle.

Tomnaverie Stone Circle (near Tarland, *Aberdeenshire*)

This recumbent stone circle is approximately 4000 years old.

Torhouse Stone Circle (near Wigtown, *Dumfries and Galloway*)

This Bronze Age recumbent stone circle has nineteen boulders lying on the edge of a low mound. This type of stone circle is more commonly found in the northeast of Scotland.

Torrylin Cairns (near Blackwaterfoot, Arran, *North Ayrshire*)

Lying in the southwest of the island, Torrylin is a Neolithic chambered cairn inside which skeletal remains and a flint knife were found.

Totnes Castle (Totnes, *Devon*)

This motte-and-bailey castle is a fine example of Norman fortification.

Tower of London (City of London, *London*)

Although usually regarded as a place of imprisonment and death, the Tower had various uses, ranging from royal residence to repository of the Crown's treasure. It was originally built as a fort by William the Conqueror. By 1100 it had grown into a vast palace-fortress, dominated by the central White Tower. Henry VI is said to have been buried in the Chapel of St John after his murder in 1471. Tower Green surrounds the White Tower, and this is where the executions of some traitors took place. Others were executed in front of crowds on Tower Hill. Anne Boleyn, Lady Jane Grey, Catherine Howard and Sir Thomas More are among the noble Tower prisoners who are buried in the Chapel of St Peter-ad-Vincula. The Tower is famous for its black ravens, whose presence is believed to guarantee its invincibility.

The Jewel House holds the Crown Jewels. The Bloody Tower is believed to have been where Richard III murdered his nephews and where Sir Walter Raleigh spent thirteen years in captivity.

Townend (Troutbeck, Windermere, *Cumbria*)

This is an exceptional relic of life in the Lake District in centu-

ries past. It was originally built by a statesman (a wealthy yeo-
man farmer) in 1626.

Town of Ramsgate Public House (Docklands, London)

The garden of this historic riverside pub has a post where condemned pirates and thieves were chained up until the tide
washed over them three times. The post can be seen at low
tide. The pub's cellars were used as dungeons for convicts
waiting to be deported to Australia.

Town Walls Tower (Shrewsbury, *Shropshire*)

This is the last remaining watchtower and it was built in the
14th century.

Trafalgar Square (West End, London)

The statue of Admiral Horatio Nelson was errected here in the
late 18th century after Nelson's naval defeat of Napoleon at
the Battle of Trafalgar in 1805.

Traquair House (near Peebles, *Scottish Borders*)

Dating from the 10th century, this is one of Scotland's oldest
inhabited houses. Twenty-seven Scottish and English monarchs have stayed at this house. At the end of one of Traquair
House's parallel drives is a set of gates that are permanently
closed. They were closed behind Bonnie Prince Charlie after
he left the house in the autumn of 1745 as the fifth Earl wished
him luck and vowed never to open the gates again until a
Stuart was on the throne.

Tredegar House (Newport, *Newport*)

This was home to one of the most important Welsh families,
the Morgans, later Lords Tredegar for over 500 years. It is one
of the most magnificent 17th-century houses that can be seen
in Britain.

Tregiffan Burial Chamber (St Buryan, *Cornwall*)

This chambered tomb is thought to be Neolithic or Bronze Age.

Trendle Ring *see* BICKNOLLER HILL.

Tre'r Ceiri (near Llanaelhaern, *Gwynedd*)
This Iron Age hillfort is surrounded by massive walls measuring 4.5 metres (15 feet) thick.

Trethevy Quoit (St Cleer, *Cornwall*)
This ancient Neolithic burial chamber consists of five standing stones that are surmounted by a huge capstone.

Tretower Castle (Tretower, *Powys*)
A motte-and-bailey castle was established here during the Norman conquest of Brycheiniog. A shell-keep was built on the mound in 1150 and a round tower was added in the early 13th century.

Tretower Court (Tretower, *Powys*)
Dating from the 15th century, this restored courtyard house has magnificent surviving timberwork in the northern and western ranges.

Tron Steeple (City of Glasgow)
This forms an arch over the pavement and is the only remnant of a 1637 church that was accidently burnt down in the late 18th century by drunken members of the local Hell Fire Club.

Trumpan (Trumpan, Isle of Skye, *Highland*)
The ruined church was the site of a 1579 fight between the MacLeods and the MacDonalds. All but one of the MacLeods, who were worshipping in the church, were killed by the invading MacDonalds. The surviving MacLeod raised the alarm, and all the MacDonalds were in turn killed by the rest of the clan MacLeod.

Tudor Merchant's House *see* TENBY TUDOR MERCHANT'S HOUSE.

Tullaghoge Fort (Cookstown, *County Londonderry*)
This large hill-top earthwork was once the headquarters of the O'Hagans, chief justices of the old kingdom of Tyrone. The O'Neill chiefs of Ulster were crowned here between the 12th and 16th centuries. The king elect was seated on a stone inau-

guration chair and new sandals were placed on his feet before he was anointed and crowned. The last such ceremony to take place here was held in the 1590s. Lord Mountjoy ordered the destruction of the stone throne in 1600.

Tullibardine Chapel (near Crieff, *Perth and Kinross*)

This is one of the most complete small medieval churches in Scotland. It was founded in 1446 and was largely rebuilt around 1500.

Tully Castle (Derrygonnelly, *County Fermanagh*)

This Scottish-style strong house was built by Sir John Hume in the early 17th century. The castle was captured and most of its inhabitents slaughtered by the Maguires in the 1641 Rising. Extensive ruins can be seen at this site today.

Turin Hill (near Forfar, *Angus*)

This Iron Age hillfort, known as Kemp's Castle, was originally a large enclosure with two ramparts surrounded by a stone wall. It was replaced by three duns later in the Iron Age.

Tutbury (Tutbury, *Derbyshire*)

The town is overlooked by the ruins of a 12th-century castle where Mary Queen of Scots was twice held prisoner.

Twelve Apostles' Stone Circle (near Dumfries, *Dumfries and Galloway*)

This stone circle dated to 2000 BC is the largest diameter stone circle in Scotland. Only eleven of the stones remain.

Ty Mawr Wybrnant (near Betws-y-coed, *Gwynedd*)

This was the birthplace of Bishop William Morgan in 1545. He was the first man to translate the Bible into Welsh.

Tynan Village Cross *see* VILLAGE CROSS.

Tynemouth Priory Castle (Tynemouth, *Tyne and Wear*)

The gatehouse and castle walls enclose the substantial remains of a Benedictine priory that was founded in 1090 on a Saxon monastic site.

U

Uffington Castle, White Horse and Dragon Hill (near Wantage, *Oxfordshire*)

This group of sites lies along the Ridgeway, an old prehistoric route. There is a large Iron Age camp that is enclosed within ramparts, a natural mound known as Dragon Hill, and a White Horse cut from the turf to reveal the chalk below.

Uley Long Barrow (near Dursley, *Gloucestershire*)

The mound of this Neolithic chambered burial mound, dating from 3000 BC, is still intact.

Unstan Chambered Cairn (near Stromness, *Orkney*)

At this Neolithic site a mound covers a stone burial chamber that is divided into five compartments by slabs.

Upnor Castle (Upnor, *Kent*)

This well-preserved 16th-century gun fort was built to protect the warships of Queen Elizabeth I. However, in 1667 the Dutch navy were able to overcome English defences and stormed up the Medway to destroy half the English fleet.

Upper Plym Valley (near Yelverton, *Devon*)

Six square miles of ancient Dartmoor landscape are covered with prehistoric and medieval sites at this important site.

Urquhart Castle (near Drumnadrochit, *Highland*)

Standing on the shores of Loch Ness, this is one of the largest castles in Scotland. It fell into decay in 1689. The tower is the best-preserved area of the castle and dates from the 16th century, as do most of the other remains.

U. S. Grant Ancestral Homestead (Ardboe, *County Tyrone*)

This was the ancestral homestead of Ulysses S. Grant, the 18th president of the United States of America.

Usk Castle (Usk, *Monmouthshire*)
  A ruined 12th-century castle dominates the small village of Usk.

V

Valle Crucis Abbey (near Llangollen, *Denbighshire*)
  This Cistercian abbey was founded in 1201. The extensive remains include the church, which dates from the 13th century, and the cloister, which was remodelled in the 14th century.

Village Cross (Tynan, *County Armagh*)
  This carved High Cross is 3 metres (11 feet) high. It lay broken in two pieces for many years but was repaired in 1844. The carvings depict the story of Adam and Eve.

Vindolanda Fort (near Twice Brewed, *Northumberland*)
  At this site on HADRIAN'S WALL there are the remains of a fort and a well-excavated civil settlement.

W

Wade's Causeway (near Pickering, *North Yorkshire*)
  This is the best-preserved stretch of Roman roadway in Britain. It was built around AD 80 and was once 25 miles (40 kilometres) long. Today just over 1 mile (1.6 kilometres) remains. The gravel surface has gone, but the slabs and kerbstones remain.

Wadebridge (Wadebridge, *Cornwall*)
  Built in 1485, this is the oldest working road bridge in Britain, the piers of which are said to be built on woolpacks.

Wallog (Wallog, *Powys*)
  A finger of shingle that stretches out from the beach is said to

be the dyke of Cantef-y-Gwaelod, the legendary drowned city that is said to lie beneath Cardigan Bay.

Wall Roman Site (Wall, near Lichfield, *Staffordshire*)

At this site there are the remains of a staging post and the foundations of an inn and bath house.

Walls, The (York, *North Yorkshire*)

Built by Henry III in 1220, these walls stretch for 3 miles (4.8 kilometres) and have four principal gateways and thirty-nine towers.

Walltown Crags (near Greenhead, *Northumberland*)

This is one of the best-preserved sections of HADRIAN'S WALL.

Walmer Castle (near Walmer, *Kent*)

This was one of the many forts built in the 16th century by Henry VIII to protect the south coast of England. It was designed to cope with the new threat of gunpowder attacks, and the design is quite different from that of a traditional medieval castle. It is low to the ground and squat and has extremely thick walls designed to be able to withstand the mightiest bombardment. The bastions held heavy armament which could be deployed against attacking forces.

The castle was later converted into a stately home to serve as a residence for the Lords Warden of the Cinque Ports. Previous Wardens have included William Pitt the Younger, Sir Winston Churchill and the Duke of Wellington.

Waltham Abbey Gatehouse and Bridge (Waltham Abbey, *Essex*)

This abbey was founded in 1030 by King Harold. 'Harold's Bridge', part of the abbey's cloister and a large 14th-century gatehouse can all be seen at this site.

Warkworth Castle (Warkworth, *Northumberland*)

This is one of the finest examples of an aristocrat's fortified residence in Britain. It acted as a defence against sieges and attacks and as a home to the most powerful family in the north, the Percys. The massive defences were begun in the 12th century after the area was regained from the Scots. The castle was granted to the Percy family in the 14th century, and it was this that ensured its stature. The Percys were able to build a castle strong enough to withstand the mightiest of enemies and protected it with a huge curtain wall surmounted with towers at each corner. The castle was built in stages, and additions were made when time and money permitted. In the late 14th century the great keep was added. This was in effect a second castle and became the new family residence.

The most famous Percy to inhabit Warkworth Castle was Harry Hotspur (Sir Henry Percy) who, along with his father, the Earl of Northumberland, dominated the borders in the 15th century. He initially fought on the side of the King against the Scots but was later instrumental in the removal of Richard II from the throne.

Warton Old Rectory (Warton, *Lancashire*)

The ruins of this rare medieval stone house include the remains of the hall, chambers and domestic offices.

Warwick Castle (Warwick, *Warwickshire*)

This was the most magnificient of the fedual mansions of the English aristocracy and is still inhabited. The curtain wall and massive tower, dating from the 14th century and are intact. The great hall dates from the 16th century.

Washington Old Hall (Washington, *Tyne and Wear*)

This was the family home of George Washington's ancestors. It remained in the family until 1613.

Waverly Abbey (near Farnham, *Surrey*)

Founded in 1128, this was the first Cistercian house in England. The ruins that remain date from the 13th century.

Wayland's Smithy (near Ashbury, *Oxfordshire*)

This Neolithic burial site is surrounded by a small circle of trees. This site has two grave types lying one upon the other, which is unusual.

Weeting Castle (near Brandon, *Norfolk*)

The ruins of this medieval manor house stand within the confines of a shallow, rectangular moat.

Well of Lecht (near Tomintoul, *Moray*)

At this site there is a carved stone monument to General Wade and the team of soldier-builders who built military roads to open up the Highlands in the 18th century in order to 'pacify' the local population.

Wells Cathedral (Wells, *Somerset*)

This is one of the most magnificent cathedrals in England. It was built between the 12th and 14th centuries. It is 127 metres (415 feet) long, with a transept measuring 47 metres (155 feet), a central tower of 47 metres (155 feet) and two western towers each 38 metres (126 feet) high.

Wenlock Priory (Much Wenlock, *Shropshire*)

The ruins of this large Cluniac priory include the substantial remains of the early 13th-century church and the Norman chapterhouse.

Weobley Castle (near Llanrhidian, *Swansea*)

This medieval fortified manor house has substantial remains dating from the late 13th and 14th centuries.

Western Heights (Dover, *Kent*)

At this site it is possible to see parts of the moat of a 19th-century fort that was built to fend off a French attack.

West Kennet Avenue (Avebury, *Wiltshire*)

This avenue of standing stones once ran in a curve from AVEBURY STONE CIRCLES to The SANCTUARY and is thought to date from the late Neolithic Age.

West Kennet Long Barrow (near West Kennet, *Wiltshire*)

This Neolithic chambered tomb consists of a long earthen

mound that contains a passage with side chambers. The entrance is guarded by a large stone.

Westminster Abbey (Westminster, London)

The original abbey was built in 1050 by King Edward the Confessor to replace the small, timber church of St Peter's. William the Conqueror was crowned here in 1066, and since then rulers of England have always been crowned here. The buildings that can be seen today were constructed between the 13th and 16th centuries. Here stands the Coronation Chair, which was made in the reign of Edward II to hold the Scottish Stone of Destiny, whidh had been seized in 1297 by Edward I. It was returned to Scotland in 1996. There are the tombs of many medieval kings and queens here as well as the tombs of Henry VII, Mary Tudor and Elizabeth I.

West Port (St Andrews, *Fife*)

This is one of the few surviving city gates in Scotland. It was built in 1589 and renovated in 1843.

West Wycombe (West Wycombe, *Buckinghamshire*)

This village is made up of fine house dating from the 15th to 18th centuries. The hill-top church, built on the site of an Iron-Age fort, is surmounted by a golden ball and was the meeting place of the notorious Hell Fire Club—a fraternity of knights founded by Sir Francis Dashwood. Dashwood built the mausoleum in 1763 and West Wycombe Park mansion in 1750.

Wetheral Priory Gatehouse (Wetheral, *Cumbria*)

The gatehouse of this Benedictine priory was preserved after the dissolution of the monasteries by serving as the vicarage for the parish church.

Wharram Deserted Village (near Malton, *North Yorkshire*)

This is one of over three thousand deserted medieval villages to have been identified from outlines of walls and foundations. At this site the remains of a medieval church still stand.

Wheeldale Roman Road (near Goathland, *North Yorkshire*)
This stretch of Roman road measuring 1 mile (1.6 kilometres) long still has its hard core and drainage ditches.

Whispering Men, The *see* ROLLRIGHT STONES.

Whitby Abbey (Whitby, *North Yorkshire*)
This abbey, situated in a spectacular cliff-top setting, contained the shrine of St Hilda, who founded the abbey in 657 and died in 680. The abbey was destroyed by Viking invaders in 867, rebuilt by the Norman invader Reinfid in the late 1070s, rebuilt in the 1220s and then dismantled in 1538 under the reign of Henry VIII.

Whitchurch Canonicorum (near Bridport, *Devon*)
This is the only English parish church that claims to house the bones of its patron saint. The remains of St Whit are said to be kept inside a tomb that has been pierced by holes. Medieval pilgrims used to place crippled limbs through these holes in the hope that they would be cured.

Whitebridge (near Loch Ness, *Highland*)
This humpback bridge is no longer in use but was built by General Wade over the River Fechlin in 1732 in order to move forces against Jacobite rebels.

White Castle (near Abergavenny, *Monmouthshire*)
This ruined 12th-century moated stronghold was built by Henry de Burgh to defend the Welsh Marches. The remains include parts of the walls, towers and a gatehouse. This is the finest of the three 'trilateral' castles built by de Burgh, the others being GROSMONT and SKENFIRTH CASTLES.

White Caterthun *see* CATERTHUNS.

White Cottage *see* DUNHAM MASSEY.

White Island Church (Castle Archdale Bay, *County Fermanagh*)
This small, roofless 12th-century church has eight unusual stone carved figures lined up on its far wall. The figures are

part pagan and part Christian in appearance and there has been a great deal of speculation about their significance. The church stands on the site of an early monastic site.

White Ladies Priory (near Boscobel House, *Shropshire*)

At this site it is possible to see the ruins of a late 12th-century church of a small priory of Augustinian canonesses.

Whitely Castle (near Alston, *County Durham*)

This was a Roman fort that was built in the 2nd century and rebuilt in the 3rd century. All that remains today is a complex system of ditches.

Whitesands Bay (near St David's, *Pembrokeshire*)

A memorial tablet marks the site of the chapel of St Patrick who is said to have sailed to Ireland from here.

Whithorn Priory (Whithorn, *Dumfries and Galloway*)

Whithorn is the cradle of Christianity in Scotland and was first founded in the 5th century by St Ninian. The priory for Premonstratensian canons was built in the 12th century by Fergus, Lord of Galloway, and it later became the cathedral church of Galloway.

Wichenford Dovecote (Wichenford, *Hereford and Worcester*)

This is a 17th-century half-timbered dovecote.

Wideford Hill Chambered Cairn (near Kirkwall, *Orkney*)

This fine Neolithic chambered cairn has three concentric walls and a large burial chamber that has three large cells.

Wigmore Castle (near Leominster, *Hereford and Worcester*)

This site has been fortified since the 1060s, and the present ruins date from the 13th and 14th centuries. The castle was dismantled during the Civil War and has been largely untouched since then.

Willington Dovecote and Stables (Willington, *Bedfordshire*)

At this site it is possible to see 16th-century stables and a dovecote, also 16th century, lined with 1500 nesting boxes.

Willowford Wall, Turrets and Bridge (near Gilsland, *Northumberland*)

This 914-metre (1000-yard) section of HADRIAN'S WALL has two turrets leading to bridge abutment remains.

Winchester Cathedral (Winchester, *Hampshire*)

This cathedral was founded in 1079 and was built adjacent to the site of the first minster to be built in Winchester in the 7th century by the Saxon king, Cenealh. The building of the cathedral lasted 300 years, so it represents a variety of styles, ranging from early Norman to Perpendicular. The nave measures 169 metres (556 feet), making it the longest medieval church in Europe. King Canute's mortuary chest lies above the high altar and William II's lies in the presbytery. Saint Swithun's tomb is in the Norman crypt, although it was originally buried outside. Legend tells that St Swithun was so angry about being moved to where 'the rain of heaven' could not fall on him that he took his revenge by making it rain for forty days.

Winchester Great Hall (Winchester, *Hampshire*)

This is the sole remnant of the castle that was begun in 1067 and rebuilt by Henry III. The Tudors regarded this as King Arthur's Camelot, and there is a wooden disc that is said to have been Arthur's Round Table. It probably dates from the 14th century. In 1603, Sir Walter Raleigh heard his death sentence here.

Winchester Palace (Southwark, London)

The remains of this 13th-century town house, which belonged to the Bishops of Winchester, include the west gable end of the Great Hall, which has an unusual round window. Winchester Palace was badly damaged by a fire in 1814.

Windmill Hill (near Avebury, *Wiltshire*)

The remains of three Neolithic concentric rings of ditches can be seen at this site.

Windsor Castle (Windsor, *Berkshire*)

The castle, which was originally constructed in wood by William the Conqueror, is still a royal residence and claims to be the world's largest inhabited fortress. The castle was rebuilt in stone by Henry II, and it was extensively restored during the reign of George IV.

Wingfield Manor (near Derby, *Derbyshire*)

This huge, ruined country manor house was where Mary Queen of Scots was imprisoned in 1569. It has not been occupied since the 1770s but the late-Gothic Great Hall and High Tower indicate the importance of Wingfield Manor in its heyday.

Winshields Wall (near Haltwhistle, *Northumberland*)

This rugged section of HADRIAN'S WALL includes the highest point, which is at Winshields Crag.

Winterbourne Poor Lot Barrows (near Winterbourne Abbas, *Dorset*)

This is part of an extensive Bronze Age cemetery thought to be 4000 years old.

Woden Law (near Jedburgh, *Scottish Borders*)

This 423-metre (1388-foot) hill top once had Roman legions stationed on it. Prior to that it was inhabited by Iron Age people.

Wolvesey Castle (Old Bishop's Palace) (Wolvesey, *Hampshire*)

This is one of the greatest medieval buildings in England. The Bishops of Winchester had the Palace as their chief residence. The ruins that can be seen today reflect the importance and wealth of the Palace's inhabitants. The wedding breakfast of Queen Mary and Philip of Spain on 25 July 1554 was the last great occasion that took place here.

Woodhenge (near Amesbury, *Wiltshire*)

This Neolithic ceremonial monument is thought to date from

2300 BC and consists of a bank and ditch and six concentric rings of timber posts. The entrance and long axis of the oval ring points to the rising sun on Midsummer Day. it was contemporary with the first stage of STONHENGE.

Woolsthorpe Manor (Woolsthorpe-by-Colsterworth, *Lincolnshire*)

This small 17th-century farmhouse was the birthplace and family home of Sir Isaac Newton. In the orchard there is a descendant of the famous apple tree.

Wordsworth House (Cockermouth, *Cumbria*)

This north-country Georgian town house was built in 1745 and was where William Wordsworth was born in 1770.

Wroxeter Roman City (Wroxeter, *Shropshire*)

At this site it is possible to see the excavated centre of the fourth largest city in Roman Britain. There are impressive remains of 2nd-century municipal baths.

Y

Yarmouth Castle (Yarmouth, *Isle of Wight*)

This, the last of Henry VIII's additions to coastal defences, was completed in 1547.

Yarnbury Castle (near Stonehenge, *Wiltshire*)

The entrance to this Iron Age hillfort is reached through double-earth ramparts.

Yarn Market (Dunster, *Somerset*)

This is an octagonal 17th-century market hall.

Y Gaer (near Brecon, *Powys*)

The Romans built their great fort here in AD 75. It was the largest of its type in Wales and covered 5 acres.

Y Gaer Fawr and Y Gaer Fach (Carn Goch, near Llandeilo, *Carmarthenshire*)

Y Gaer Fawr, 'the big fort', was used to house the tribe and cattle of an Iron Age settlement. Y Gaer Fach, 'the small fort', was an outer defence.

Y Pigwn (near Llandovery, *Carmarthenshire*)

In about AD 50 Roman legions marched along the high track between Trecastle and Llandovery. Evidence of their camps can still be seen.

York Minster (York, *North Yorkshire*)

This is the largest medieval cathedral in England. It was founded in 1220 and took more than 250 years to build. It measures 158 metres (519 feet) long and the central roof is 60 metres (198 feet) high.

Ysbyty Cynfyn (Ysbyty Cynfyn, *Ceredigion*)

The village's 19th-century church has a churchyard with walls made from prehistoric stones and is built on the site from which they were taken.

Z

Zennor (Zennor, *Cornwall*)

This village, named after St Senara, has a Norman church that contains a seat with a legendary carved mermaid on it. To the south of the village lies Zennor Quoit, the largest Stone Age burial chamber in the country. It comprises seven stones capped by a massive slab.